APA STYLE BASICS

APA Style Basics

Writing Student Papers in Psychology and the Social Sciences

Mark Hatala, Ph.D.

Greentop Academic Press • Greentop, Missouri

Copyright ©2019 by Mark Hatala

All rights reserved under
International and Pan-American copyright conventions
Published in the United States of America
by the Greentop Academic Press, Greentop, MO 63546

(pop 427)

09 08 07 06 05 1 2 3 4 5

APA Style Basics: Writing Student Papers in Psychology and the Social Sciences by Mark Hatala, Ph.D.

Except for the quotation of short passages for the purpose of criticism and review, no part of this publication may be reproduced or transmitted, in any form or by any means, without the prior permission of the publisher.

ISBN-13: 978-1-933167-03-9
ISBN-10: 1-933167-03-3

Book Design: Charles Dunbar

The font used in this book is Times New Roman, which is the approved font of the American Psychological Association; however, the interior uses a 10-point font to save space - APA style requires a 12-point font.

To incorporate this book into your classroom, visit our website at APAcentral.com

Table of Contents

Structure of the book

Section 1 - Getting Started

Choosing the topic of your paper	13
Finding appropriate research	14
Wikipedia	14
Psychology databases	14
Google Scholar	15
Google and the web	16
Data mining from textbooks and articles	16
The bottom line	17
Types of sources	17
Primary sources	18
Secondary sources	18
Tertiary sources	18
Types of articles	19
Experiments	19
Correlational studies	20
Literature reviews	20
Meta-analysis	21
Case studies	21
Everything else	22

Section 2 - Writing Your Paper

Writing from an outline	23
Introduction	25
The Opening	25
The Thesis Statement	26
A Complete Introduction: Example	28
Body	29
Conclusions	32
References	34
Reference alphabetization	34

Section 3 - Citations

1. Types of citation - "in-text" vs. "parenthetical"	37
2. How often should you make a citation?	38
3. Is this the first time you cite the source or a subsequent time?	40
Source with one author	40
Source with two authors	41
Source with three, four, or five authors	41
Source with six or more authors	43
4. What if there are multiple sources within the same citation?	43
Multiple sources from the same author from the same year	43
Multiple sources from the same author from different years	44
Multiple sources within the same set of parentheses	44
Sources with no identifiable author	45
5. How would you cite a direct quote?	46
As cited in	49

Section 4 - References

Periodicals	51
Journal articles as references	52
Journal article with one author	52
Journal article with two authors	52
Journal article with three authors	52
Journal article with four authors	52
Journal article with five authors	52
Journal article with six authors	53
Journal article with seven authors	53
Journal article with eight or more authors	53
Magazine article - In print or online	54
Newspaper article - In print or online	54
Books	55
Book with one author	55
Book with two authors	56
Book with three authors	56
Book with four authors	56
Book chapters	56
Book chapter with one author	57
Book chapter with two authors	57
Book chapter with three authors	57
Book chapter with four authors	57
Wikipedia, encyclopedia, or reference work - In print or online	58
Wikipedia	58
Encyclopedia - in print	58

Encyclopedia - online	58
Dictionary - in print or online	59
Subject-specific reference book	59
Meetings, symposium, paper and poster presentations	60
Doctoral dissertations, master's theses, technical reports	60
Audiovisual media	61
Television show - individual episode	62
Reviews and peer commentary	62
Podcast	62
Blog post	62
Comment on a blog post	63
Video blog post	63
Music recording and music videos	63
Social media	63
Personal communications	64
Twitter	64
Facebook post	64

Section 5 - Odds and Ends

Comparing A-F student papers	65
The "A" paper - "Almost perfection"	65
The "B" paper - "A solid effort"	66
The "C" paper - "There's some good stuff here!"	66
The "D" paper - "A good rough draft"	67
The "F" paper - "Uh oh" or "See me"	68
A word about non-sexist and non-biased writing	69
A note on plagiarism	71
Setting up your paper in Microsoft Word or google docs	74

Section 6 - Do It Like This!

The mandatory A+ sample paper	75
The mandatory "journal submission"	91
APA style in a nutshell	107
APA-approved list of abbreviations	111
List of non-sexist and non-biased terms	113
References for common topics	114
Index	134

Structure of the book

This book is divided into six sections because ten is too many and three is too few. The more accurate reason is because I believe that writing is a process, and it helps to follow certain steps when you're learning a new skill. Writing a paper is like following a recipe: it can seem overwhelming at first, but when you can see it in terms of instructions and tasks, it becomes much easier.

The first section is about choosing a topic for your paper and then finding appropriate research. Types of sources and research articles are discussed, as well as the best places to find relevant studies.

The second section is about actually writing your paper. I stress the importance of writing from an outline and what to put into each paragraph of your paper. For example, the introduction of your paper begins with a hook and ends with a thesis statement. Once you have your thesis statement, the rest of the paper basically writes itself!

The third and fourth sections are on how to do citations (both in-text and parenthetical) and references. Students often find citations tricky because it can be difficult to know when to do a citation, how a subsequent citation of the same source changes, how to cite direct quotes, etc.

The fifth section is something of a "catch all" of everything else that I think is important but didn't cover earlier. So, things like the differences between A-F student papers, plagiarism, and how to be sure that your writing is non-sexist and non-biased.

The final section contains a mandatory student A+ sample paper and a journal article submission. I've always felt that sample papers are quite helpful for students because it's one thing to understand the rules of APA style, and another to apply them in an actual paper.

The book ends with some helpful appendices and references on common topics for undergraduate psychology papers.

I have posted a number of lectures about writing in APA style to both YouTube and APAcentral.com in order to help you to write the best paper you can. Good luck!

Mark Hatala, Ph.D.
Professor of Psychology
Truman State University

Section 1 - Getting Started
Choosing the topic of your paper

Most undergraduate papers in psychology are literature reviews, where the student is reading research and then reporting what they have learned and what issues are prominent in the field. This can be thought of as analogous to the introduction section of an actual research article. Since this is the kind of paper most undergraduates will be required to write, it will also be the focus of most of this book.

One issue when choosing a topic is making sure that it is not too broad. I have had student requests to study topics such as "nature versus nurture" or "serial killers;" not only are both topics too broad even for a dissertation (much less a class paper), but there is also the problem that experimental studies cannot be performed on "serial killers." As an aside, due to television and movies, many students will say that they would like to study murderers as forensic psychologists. The best advice for them is to drop psychology as a major and instead go into acting, as they are much more likely to play a "profiler" on television than they are to be one in real life.

There are a number of easy ways to narrow a topic that is too broad. One way is to narrow the topic by a demographic characteristic, such as sex, race, or age. For example, the topic of "depression" is too broad, but specifically studying research done on adolescent Hispanic women would be fine.

Clinical topics can be narrowed by therapeutic orientation. Sticking with the too broad topic of "depression," there are a number of different, specific therapies to treat and manage depression, so a paper might examine the effectiveness of one type of biomedical treatment. Bupropian, for example, is both an aid for people who are trying to quit smoking and also acts as an SSRI-based antidepressant sold under the brand names of Wellbutrin and Zyban.

Perhaps the easiest way to narrow a topic is to read more about it. The topic of "memory" is, again, far too broad, but by reading about memory in a General Psychology textbook, one can discover what research issues are prominent in the field, and can then determine a more specific, appropriate topic, such as context-dependent memory, the effect of mood on recall, naps and memory consolidation, or literally hundreds of other possible paper topics.

An opposite problem is when the topic is just too specific. Again, many students who are interested in "serial killers" have a particular serial killer in mind, like Jeffrey Dahmer or Ted Bundy, but since there is no experimental research on these people, the research trail comes to a dead end. However, serial killers like Dahmer and Bundy were clearly "psychopaths" or "sociopaths" (terms no longer in clinical use), and there is plenty of research on people with antisocial personality disorder (ASPD). A book which examines this research is *The Wisdom of Psychopaths: What Saints, Spies, and Serial Killers Can Teach Us About Success* by Kevin Dutton. From Dutton's book, actual psychological research studies on topics like empathy and the "trolley problem" are discussed, and the original research articles are listed in the appendix of the book. In this way, a topic that may appear too specific can be broadened to an acceptable idea for a paper. It just takes a change in perspective.

Finding appropriate research

Wikipedia

Let's face it, most research starts out on the web, and inevitably ends up at Wikipedia. Using Wikipedia as a reference in your paper tells your professor "I didn't try, and I don't care," but specific topics are usually based on cited research, and the citations are referenced at the bottom of the Wikipedia webpage. For example, the topic of context-dependent memory was mentioned earlier, and a visit to the Wikipedia page reveals 56(!) research articles on the topic - articles that can be incorporated into a student research paper.

The problem with Wikipedia is that it is written by volunteers who contribute to the content on a particular topic, and like much in life, you often get what you pay for. The contributors are not necessarily experts in the field, and the research they cite may be obscure or controversial. Since you are unfamiliar with the topic (which is why you're reading about it on Wikipedia) it can be difficult to determine what research is important and what is not. So Wikipedia can play a role in finding appropriate research (to be discussed below), but if it is the "one stop shop" of your research, you are likely to encounter problems later.

PsycARTICLES, PsycINFO, and Psychology Collection

A different (although not necessarily "better") way to find research articles is through online databases, which are usually available through academic libraries. Three common psychology databases are PsycARTICLES, PsycINFO, and Psychology Collection.

PsycARTICLES and PsycINFO are both published by the American Psychological Association (otherwise known as the APA) and differ in the level of access they provide. PsycINFO searches much more broadly (literally millions of articles, dissertations, theses, papers, etc.), but often provides only the abstract (or summary) of an article. PsycARTICLES provides full text for articles published by the APA, but only searches the 90 journals that are part of this database. Since both PsycINFO and PsycARTICLES are published by the APA, all of the information in PsycARTICLES is redundant with PsycINFO, which means that anything that can be found in PsycARTICLES will also be found (including the full-text component) in PsycINFO. So why bother using PsycARTICLES at all? Good question! Personally, I like to know that I am going to be able to find a full-text version of any article I find interesting, so I tend to use PsycARTICLES for my initial search, and then PsychINFO to be sure that I did not miss any other particularly relevant articles.

Psychology Collection is owned by the educational publishing company Gale, which is in turn owned by the larger textbook publishing company Cengage (which is undoubtedly owned by someone else). It provides a database search in the same way as PsycINFO and PsycARTICLES, except that Psychology Collection also includes articles published in magazines, newspapers, and books. Does that make it more inclusive than the APA-published databases? Surprisingly, no, and I will provide an example of this in a moment. While one would think that a database is a database is a database, and they are all using the same search information, this is not true.

An interesting way of examining this is through some research on context-dependent memory and chewing gum (chewing gum!) that was done in the late 2000s. Searching each database with the exact same terms ("context-dependent memory" and "chewing gum") leads to different results. For example, PsycINFO, which is the most inclusive database, contains six articles published between 2004 and 2013 (two of which are full-text), when this was apparently a hotbed of intensive research. Psychology Collection contains two articles; one was in the PsychINFO output and the other is from a Spanish-language Latin American research journal (specifically, *Avances en Psicologia Latinoamericana*). PsycARTICLES provides no results (and probably is judging you for searching such an obscure topic) because none of the research published on the topic of context-dependent memory and chewing gum ever appeared in an APA-published journal. So, to conclude, PsycINFO was the most inclusive database and provided the largest number of pertinent results. Psychology Collection provided, at best, an incomplete survey of the research (although it did find an obscure Spanish-language publication) and PsycARTICLES provided no results at all. This is why it is important to use multiple means for acquiring research articles for your paper.

Google Scholar - An alternative to Google

What about Google Scholar? It's clearly more scientific than just googling your topic because it contains the word "scholar," which means "someone who is highly educated." I know this because I googled the definition of the word "scholar."

Google Scholar (scholar.google.com) is an even broader database than PsycARTICLES, PsycINFO, and the Psychology Collection, and includes cross-disciplinary research that may not appear in the psychology databases. Interestingly (although perhaps not relevantly), Google Scholar also contains web sites, court cases, and other arcane sources.

So how does it do with the search of "context-dependent memory" and "chewing gum?" Google Scholar finds several of the same articles as PsycINFO (and also misses the Spanish-language Latin American research journal), but it also includes an unpublished, uncited research paper from 2016 that was not included in any of the other databases. Is the unpublished research paper "good?" Probably not, because it has not been published in a peer-reviewed journal and has been cited by no other researchers. This means that it's about as valid a research article as something someone just puts up on their webpage, although to be fair, at least it's written by people with an academic affiliation. Are they professors? Are they students? There's no way to tell, so it's best to just stick to research that has been published in research journals and cited by other researchers.

Overall, my belief is that Google Scholar is redundant with the psychology databases, but I don't think you're making a mistake by using it to check for interdisciplinary articles and websites related to your topic. For the amount of time it takes (less than a minute) and its world-wide availability (you need access to an academic library to use the psychology databases), Google Scholar is worth consulting. However, by this point you might be thinking . . .

"Forget all those databases! I'll just google my topic, thank you!"

From a professor's perspective, using google to research your topic shows that you were not even motivated enough to go to Wikipedia. I once had a student try to convince me that they would be able to construct an entire paper about Tsutomu Yamaguchi (a man who had survived nuclear bomb blasts at both Hiroshima and Nagasaki) from "facts" they had obtained from the Cracked.com website. I was able to convince the student that this was a poor choice, and they moved on to a different topic, but even if they had gone to Wikipedia, they would have found over 25 sources about the life of this otherwise obscure man.

There are times when information from a website may be the most up-to-date source for a particular topic. Information from sources like the Mayo Clinic (mayoclinic.org) and the Centers for Disease Control and Prevention (cdc.gov) are credible and cover a variety of scientific topics. I also admit to having a soft spot for Science Blogs (scienceblogs.com) and the brilliant Cecil Adams at The Straight Dope (straightdope.com). These websites are best used in guiding paper writers to primary sources rather than serving as sources themselves.

To go back to the earlier example of context-dependent memory and chewing gum (now for the fifth time), you get the same results that were provided by Google Scholar, but in a different format. Further, a google search of just "context-dependent memory" provides a definition from the Wikipedia page devoted to the topic, so in a very meta sense, we are back where we started.

Data mining from textbooks and research articles

The truth is that someone with a Ph.D. has already done your literature search for you - the people who write research articles and textbooks. Authors of academic works cite the research that is relevant to their topic, and these are easily found in the reference section of a paper or a textbook.

As mentioned earlier, one of the problems for students is knowing whether a particular article is important or not; the more formal term in academia would be an article's "impact score." Textbooks solve this problem because they follow a familiar pattern when discussing a topic in psychology - they cite the foundational research for a particular topic, and then follow that up with more recent research on the same topic. As a student, you can simply find the reference that the textbook author cited and use those articles to guide your research.

When you find the research articles from your textbook, you will find that they ALSO cite relevant research on the topic you are interested in! Now go find those articles, and you have all of the relevant research for your paper.

This method is a gift that just keeps on giving because it creates a positive feedback loop of published researchers doing your work for you. It frees you from having to determine whether an article is "important" or not, and it provides a wide range of relevant research articles to choose from. Your professor will know what research is important, and by using this method to find articles, you won't be blindsided by them asking, "Why didn't you use the most famous article on this topic in your paper?!"

If there is a problem with this method, it is that the articles you obtain through textbooks (and even research articles) are unlikely to be the most up-to-date research on the topic. They also tend to be very broad and general, and your paper needs to be narrow and specific because you're writing a paper for class and not a dissertation for a Ph.D. So what's the answer?

The bottom line

I believe that incorporating all of the above methods is the best and most exhaustive way of finding appropriate research on your topic. Use Wikipedia to help find a topic that is interesting for you, yet narrow enough to do a paper about. Then find a general psychology textbook (or even better, a more specific textbook on abnormal, cognitive, social, I/O, etc. psychology) and see what research they cite on the topic. Read through the articles cited in the textbooks using the full-text feature available through the psychology databases and Google Scholar to find even more articles on your topic. The databases also provide an advantage in allowing you to search for more recent research than what has appeared in the textbooks. In this way, all of your bases are covered.

At this point, stop! You could spend a lifetime reading research on a particular topic, and this is why so many people have a problem finishing their graduate education - there always seems to be another relevant article left to read. Perhaps, but you also need to know when to stop. When you reach the number of articles your professor wants in your paper, find two or three more (to show your diligence as a thorough researcher) and then stop.

A final web search on your specific topic can also be beneficial because you might find something very new on your topic that even your professor was not aware of, but I said that you should stop, and so I'll stop too.

Types of sources

Now that you have your research articles, it would be helpful to take a minute to discuss the three different types of published research, and where you want to put the focus for your paper. It's important to remember that science advances through the publication process, and that scientists build on the work of others in the same field. As Isaac Newton said in 1675, "If I have seen further it is by standing on the shoulders of giants."

The sources of the research you use are important and your professor will have an idea of how hard you worked on your paper simply by looking at your reference page. If you have used a number of research articles, that is outstanding; websites and Wikipedia, not so much. There are three levels of sources: primary, secondary, and tertiary.

Primary sources

Primary sources deal with original scientific research, and are usually presented in research journals. This research has been thoroughly examined and vetted by professional academic reviewers and editors for merit and originality. They have chosen to publish the article because they believe it is scholarly, significant, and an important contribution to the field. You can identify a primary source because it will have the usual sections of a research article: introduction, method, results, and discussion. Professors prefer you to use primary sources in your paper because then they know that you have read research that others in the field consider to be important. Here is an example of a primary source reference on the topic of memory and mood:

Corson, Y., & Verrier, N. (2007). Emotions and false memories: Valence or arousal? *Psychological Science, 18*(3), 208-211.

Secondary sources

Secondary sources are chapters in edited books (more common for a specific research topic) and academic books. These books are commonly on a specific research topic such as the treatment of depression or eyewitness testimony or about a thousand other possible topics. Original research may be presented in this way, but review and analysis of previously published research is much more common. With secondary sources, you can assume that the writers and editors have published in the topic area before and are very familiar with the issues in the field that they are covering. Academic books are outstanding sources for student research papers because they often bring together a number of research papers (as edited chapters) on a very specific topic. For example, reminiscence has been used as a therapeutic technique with older people, but it is too limited of a topic to have a journal devoted to it; however, a book of review articles on the topic of reminiscence by researchers working in the field is appropriate and useful. Even though I've been talking about reminiscence, here's an example of a secondary source reference on the topic of mood and memory:

Guenther, K. (1988). Mood and memory. In G. M. Davies & D. M. Thomson (Eds.), *Memory in context: Context in memory* (pp. 58-75). Chichester, UK: Wiley.

Tertiary sources

Tertiary sources are the furthest removed from the actual research, and examples would include textbooks (which, as discussed above, are a good source for finding primary sources), newspaper or magazine articles, or websites. Although textbooks go through a vetting process (meaning that professionals in the field read, review, and revise them), they are alone in this among tertiary sources. Anything can be asserted in a newspaper, magazine, or website, and the "experts" who are interviewed may have dubious credentials and experience. On the other hand, information published in major periodicals such as the *New York Times* or the *Wall Street Journal*, or websites such as the Centers for Disease Control and Prevention (cdc.gov) or the Mayo Clinic (mayoclinic.org) can be excellent sources for the most up-to-date information on a variety of scientific topics. That's the thing about tertiary sources - they exhibit extreme variations in quality, and so should be approached with some caution.

One more thing about textbooks: although they can be an outstanding way of finding research on a particular topic, they should NOT be used in your paper itself. Using a textbook as a source is a sure way to signal to your professor that you did not take the assignment very seriously, because you did not even bother to dig very deep for sources. Personally, I equate using textbooks as sources with the same horror of students using dictionaries or encyclopedias - fine for middle or junior high school, but inappropriate for college.

An example of a source from the web (also on the topic of mood and memory) is presented below:

Munger, D. (2009, September 8). Memory and mood: Negative emotions nullify a
    problem with recall. *Science Blogs*. Retrieved from http://scienceblogs.com

Types of articles

Another consideration of some importance is the type of article that you choose to use in your paper. Basically (at least according to the APA), there are several different types of articles published in psychology journals. The types of articles that you are likely to use in your paper are experiments, correlational studies, literature reviews, meta-analyses, and case studies. There are also theoretical and methodological articles (along with a catch-all category that includes things like obituaries and book reviews), but you are unlikely to use those types of articles in your paper, although I will write about them below. To keep things clear, I will illustrate each type of article with an actual reference, and to keep things consistent, I will stick to the topic of PTSD (Post Traumatic Stress Disorder).

Experiments

Experiments take place when an independent variable (a variable which is manipulated) is introduced and a dependent variable (a variable which is measured) is observed. Experiments are viewed very favorably by researchers because they are high in internal validity, which means that they allow us to make causal statements. For example, we might provide a person with treatment for their PTSD and then measure their cortisol levels (which are related to stress). In this case, the treatment is what is being manipulated (the independent variable) and the cortisol levels are what is being measured (the dependent variable). Experiments allow us to make causal statements - treatment of PTSD leads to a lowering of cortisol levels - because the experimenter is able to control the antecedent (or prior) conditions. In other words, the experimenter determines whether the subject will participate in a treatment group or not, and the impact of that manipulation can be observed in the subject's cortisol levels.

There is also quasi-experimental research (sometimes referred to as passive research) where characteristics like sex (male or female) or handedness (left- or right-handed) are used as the independent variable. Since the researcher does not manipulate the participants' sex or handedness, the research is not considered to be a true experiment, and so it is more difficult (or even inappropriate) to make causal statements from the results.

In keeping with the research on changes in cortisol levels after successful treatment of PTSD, the following is a reference citation of such an experiment:

Pacella, M. L., Feeny, N., Zoellner, L., & Delahanty, D. L. (2014). The impact of PTSD treatment on the cortisol awakening response. *Depression and Anxiety, 31*(10), 862-869. doi:10.1002/da.22298

Correlational studies

If there is one thing that every student is taught about correlation, it is that "correlation does not imply causation." Again, it is only through experiments that we are able to make causal statements; however, correlational studies are statistically powerful and compelling, and are considered to be empirical studies by the APA.

Basically, the goal of correlational studies is to determine whether a relationship exists between two (or more) variables, and what the strength of that relationship is. For example, there is a correlation between height and weight - in general, someone who is six feet tall is heavier than someone who is five feet tall. This would be a direct (or positive) correlation: as one variable increases (height) the other variable increases (weight).

Correlational studies are outstanding for studying variables that we cannot manipulate for practical or ethical reasons. The following is a reference citation of a correlational study evaluating the relationship between religiosity, PTSD and depressive symptoms:

Tran, C. T., Kuhn, E., Walser, R. D., & Drescher, K. D. (2012). The relationship between religiosity, PTSD, and depressive symptoms in veterans in PTSD residential treatment. *Journal of Psychology & Theology, 40*(4), 313-322.

Literature Reviews

Literature reviews are articles which examine previously published research in order to critically evaluate the findings and perhaps present new interpretations of the research. They can be invaluable for students in providing an overview of the issues within a particular field of study because they are often comprehensive in scope. They can also help in narrowing a topic because students can examine one particular area of a larger topic that is of interest to them. Finally, literature reviews can provide a large number of relevant research articles based on the sources they reference.

Literature reviews tend to be fairly straightforward, and are easier to read and understand than experiments or correlational studies. The following reference citation succinctly deals with the broad topic of the pharmacological treatment of PTSD:

Steckler, T., & Risbrough, V. (2012). Pharmacological treatment of PTSD – Established and new approaches. *Neuropharmacology, 62*(2), 617-627.

Meta-analysis

Meta-analysis is considered to be a type of literature review, but with an empirical twist - it is a study of studies. That might sound like a trick, but instead of just evaluating the findings of other research like a literature review, a meta-analysis is a statistical technique where the data from multiple studies are collated in order to increase the amount of data available to the researchers. This increases the statistical power of the research because instead of having one study with 100 participants, you now have access to ten studies with 1000 participants.

Meta-analysis is not an experimental research technique (even though it is made up of experiments) because it incorporates articles which often use different methodologies, independent and dependent variables, and populations. The results are mashed together into a "statistical gumbo" designed to find significant results. Some researchers have gone as far as to say that meta-analysis is not so much "garbage in, garbage out" as it is "waste management."

Meta-analysis can be a very rewarding technique for researchers because it uses others' efforts in new ways in order to achieve statistical significance and therefore increase the likelihood of publication (which is the end goal of most academic research). Due to their data-driven, statistics-heavy nature, meta-analysis can be difficult for students not already familiar with a research area to understand the methodology and results; however, like regular old vanilla literature reviews, meta-analysis can provide a good overview of relevant research in a particular area.

The following is a reference citation of a meta-analysis dealing with the effectiveness of psychotherapy on PTSD:

Bradley, R., Jamelle, G., Eric, R., Lissa, D., & Drew, W. (2005). A multidimensional meta-analysis of psychotherapy for PTSD. *American Journal of Psychiatry, 162*(2), 214-227.

Case studies

Although they are not experimental studies, the data gathered from case studies can (and often does) lead to later experimental research. One famous psychological example of this would be the case studies that Jean Piaget did with his children in the 1920's. By studying his own three children, Piaget was able to create a psycho-social stage theory of development and generalize it to all children.

Definitionally, case studies are when one person (or a small group of people) are examined in detail by an outside observer. A second good example of this would involve the famous Sigmund Freud himself. In 1896, he published *Studies on Hysteria* with his colleague Josef Breuer, which was a series of five case studies, including the most famous patient in the history of psychoanalysis, Bertha Pappenheim (known in the book as Anna O.). Freud built his theory of psychoanalysis on evidence from case studies, and they remain a powerful source of data to this day.

Keeping with the PTSD theme, the following reference citation is a case study of three women with PTSD who were part of a larger clinical trial:

Stapleton, J. A., Taylor, S., & Asmundson, G. G. (2007). Efficacy of various treatments for PTSD in battered women: Case studies. *Journal of Cognitive Psychotherapy, 21*(1), 91-102. doi:10.1891/088983907780493287

Other types of articles

This "catch all" category is made up of things like theoretical articles, methodological articles, obituaries, letters to the editor, comments on previously published articles, and book reviews (along with anything else that does not fall into one of the categories listed above). It is very unlikely that any of these types of articles would be used in student papers because they are either too technical (theoretical or methodological articles) or too specific (everything else).

To explain more thoroughly, the purpose of a theoretical article is to present a context for advances in research, because all research needs to fit within a theoretical framework; otherwise research is just a series of studies. Methodological articles are not for the faint of heart, but are usually written for other researchers in order to introduce a new methodological or statistical technique. Again, these articles are unlikely to show up in a student paper, but the following reference citation is for a theoretical article dealing with PTSD and couples:

Beckerman, N.L. (2004). The impact of Post-Traumatic Stress Disorder on couples: A theoretical framework for assessment and intervention. *Family Therapy, 31*(3), 129-144.

Section 2 - Writing Your Paper

Now that you have collected and read all of your articles, you are ready to start writing! Academic papers tend to be very "dry" and to the point - just the facts - with little embellishment or need to speculate or entertain the reader. Student APA style papers can seem "formulaic" and that is appropriate because you are essentially writing according to a formula. The same kinds of things are expected in all papers - a thesis statement, citation of research, references, etc. Departing from the formula does not make you "creative" so much as it makes you "wrong." This is not to say that there is not wide variability in student writing, or that writing to a formula is easy. It is, however, very straightforward. I have been teaching about writing in psychology for over 25 years, and so in that time I have been able to identify the kinds of mistakes that students are likely to make, and so can be proactive in advising about "good" APA style writing. I have collected a number of student papers (along with copyright approvals) for use in teaching other students about writing. Therefore, the examples I will use are from actual student papers, and not just the "A" papers - the "F" papers too, and everything in between. These papers help to give insight into what works and what doesn't, and most importantly, how you can write the best paper possible without the workload consuming your life.

Writing from an outline

Here is a point that I cannot stress enough - write from an outline! Student APA style papers follow a basic structure of introduction, body, and conclusion. The "shape" of the paper is like an hourglass: broad at the top and more narrow in the middle. In other words, your paper should begin and end in fairly broad generalities, and discuss specific research in the middle.

I will cover each specific part of the paper below, but initially I want to make a few points in order for you to get writing.

1. Don't wait until you're in the mood to write. There are SO many distractions in life that it would be difficult to come up with something less interesting than writing your paper. College is just full of unstructured time, where you can do pretty much anything you like, and unless you enjoy writing APA style papers, you'll find something else to do. So pace yourself. Block out a half hour to write a specific section of your paper. Trying to write your entire paper in one sitting is likely to end in failure - especially if you've waited until the last moment to write it!

2. Write in haste, revise at leisure. When it comes to writing, anything is better than nothing. Once you have started writing, you can read through it and find ways to revise and make it better. If you have nothing to work with, you have nothing. Students often tell me that they "have it all worked out in their head" and they just need to commit it to paper. Forget about your head and just write it down. There is an old expression that says that the lightest ink is better than the best memory. Keep this in mind, and let your thoughts flow onto the paper.

3. Stop writing when you are "going good." This is advice from writer Ernest Hemingway, and it has always worked for me. Don't try to write your entire paper in one sitting (especially the night before it is due!). But then how do you decide where to stop? Hemingway believed that the proper time to stop was when you knew what you wanted to write about next. Since he won a Nobel Prize for Literature, I'm certainly willing to listen to him and follow his advice. Here's his full quote:

> "The best way is always to stop when you are going good and when you know what will happen next. If you do that every day when you are writing a novel you will never be stuck. That is the most valuable thing I can tell you so try to remember it."

4. Who is the audience that you are writing for? Your professor obviously, because they are the person who is going to put a grade on the paper, but does that mean that you have to write a "science-y" paper that only someone with an advanced degree will understand? Hardly! The standard advice here is to write for an educated reader who may not be familiar with the topic you are writing about. Some books on writing refer to this as a "naive reader," but I don't like that term because it makes it sound like your reader is gullible and will believe anything you put on paper.

5. There really are no "bad" papers, just papers that need further revision. Don't turn a rough draft in as your final paper. Students often dismiss their low grade on a paper by saying "I'm just not a good writer," but writing ability is not an immutable characteristic, and with proper revision, even an "F" paper can be rewritten to create an "A" paper. Write and revise. Write and revise. Some people are able to write in a way that requires less revision (they are "good writers"), but everyone can write well with some assistance. That's the entire purpose of this book!

6. Have someone else read your paper for mistakes before you turn it in. In my opinion, this should be mandatory. Why? Because although we all rely on technology to spell-check our work for us, it still takes a human reader to find all of our mistakes. I have my TAs read my work for me, and it's always head-smackingly upsetting to see how many small, easily correctable mistakes I make. And these are on manuscripts that I've already read through several times! Most schools have a "Writing Center" where you can make an appointment to have a "student peer" read your paper through for you. Take advantage of this incredibly helpful perk. If a peer reader is not available, ask a friend to read your paper. Another set of eyeballs on your work is always helpful.

Introduction

How should your paper begin? Should you start with a question (as I just did) or should you jump right into the research in order to show that you are getting down to business? I believe student introductions are best when they begin broadly and end with a thesis statement. Again, this is part of the formula for writing an APA style paper.
So how broadly should you begin? I tell students to always begin by just plugging in the phrase "People have always wondered about ____ and how it influences them and changes their lives." This phrase can pretty much go anywhere after that, and I don't want students to actually *USE* that phrase, but it acts as a placeholder in their mind of how the paper should begin. And see, you've already started writing! Begin with the universal, and then get more narrow. Again, the hourglass.

The Opening

Let me provide you with a few variations on the opening from students writing on different topics and with different grades (the grades refer to the final paper grade, and not a grade on their opening).

From an "A" paper on Generalized Anxiety Disorder:

"Nearly everyone experiences a worrisome thought from time to time, whether it is about a mortgage or a marriage. For some, however, these thoughts never end. Millions of individuals are plagued every waking moment by endless torrents of uncontrollable worry as victims of generalized anxiety disorder (GAD). The American Psychological Association (1994) describes GAD . . ."

This is good because it begins with the universal - who hasn't experienced worry? - and then becomes specific about how people with GAD are different due to their "uncontrollable worry." Is the writing too flowery? Perhaps. This is an "A" paper, not a "perfect" paper. It also uses proper citation, which will be discussed in its own section later.

From a "B" paper on the impact of breakfast on children's academic performance:

"Children everywhere have been prodded for years to eat breakfast because Tony the Tiger says it's 'G-r-r-r-eat!' The effect of breakfast on a child's behavior in school has been studied and debated for years. Many studies have . . ."

Kellogg's has literally spent millions and millions of dollars so that the allusion to Tony the Tiger is one that everyone with a pulse can recognize, so it's an effective opening. One might even say it's "g-r-r-r-eat!"

From a "C" paper on token economies in the classroom:

"Token economy has been used for quite some time but it has just been recently been utilized within the classroom setting (O'Leary & Drabman, 1971). In the classroom, it is not always simple to get children to cooperate or even behave . . ."

This paper just jumps right into it and is begging for a rewrite to "Token economies have been utilized in mental institutions for years, but have only recently been used in classroom settings (O'Leary & Drabman, 1971)." At least they use a reference, which is good, but the reference is from 1971, so that the "recently" the student is referring to is 50 years ago! The word "been" is also used three times in the first sentence! Try reading the sentence aloud. They would have been better off starting with a broader statement about how it can be difficult to get children to behave, especially in the classroom.

From a "D" paper on Munchausen Syndrome by Proxy:
"The definition of Munchausen Syndrome by Proxy is a psychological disorder in which a parent, typically a mother, harms her child by falsifying medical need and records. It is also considered a factitious disorder since the symptoms are artificially produced and do not occur naturally. The causes, symptoms, and treatments . . ."

To start, using the term "factitious disorder" without a reference is a red flag to a professor that the student is just copying straight from a source (we will talk about avoiding plagiarism later). Again, this paper just jumps right in without any introduction. It also uses no citations, not even for the "definition" of the condition being described. Also, the student did not bother to indent the paragraph, which seems to be fairly elementary.

From an "F" paper on claustrophobia:
"The walls quickly closing in, difficulty breathing, extreme anxiety leading into extreme panic attacks; These are some of the debilitating effects resulting from onset claustrophobia. Claustrophobia is the irrational fear of being in closed small spaces with no escape. This can often result in panic attacks . . ."

Ok, a number of things here. Notice that the opening is ungrammatical. Try reading it out loud. And please, know not to capitalize after a semicolon. It doesn't begin universally, and provides no citation for the assertions it makes. There is also the use of the word "claustrophobia" as the last word in one sentence, and then as the first word in the next sentence. Sloppy!

The Thesis Statement

The thesis statement provides a concise summary of what the paper is going to be about, and it appears as the last sentence of the introduction. The thesis statement is important because it informs your professor about the organization of the rest of the paper - the body of the paper will unfold from the thesis.

Again, I'm going to provide you with thesis statements from student papers so you can see the differences in clarity and proficiency:

From an "A" paper on the placebo effect:
"This paper will define the placebo effect, evaluate its efficacy as a treatment method, and examine how it is used in modern medicine."

Direct and to the point. I know exactly how the rest of the paper will unfold - define the placebo effect, evaluate how well it works, and see how it is used in medicine.

From a "B" paper on the treatment of phobias:
"The success of treatments of phobias depends on the cause of the fear, the specific form of treatment, and the autonomic flexibility of the subject."

This example puts the "statement" into "thesis statement." Because it is at the end of the introduction, I know it is their thesis statement, but it is ambiguous about what the rest of the paper will be about. Is it about the cause of the fear? What treatments are being used with people? What is "autonomic flexibility?" (the student failed to define it earlier in the introduction).

From a "C" paper on agoraphobia:
"Agoraphobia causes distress and impairs a person socially, occupationally, and educationally, but there are many treatments to prevent this anxiety (Nydegger, 2012)."

So what is this paper going to be about? Is it about how agoraphobia impairs a person "socially, occupationally, and educationally?" Will those be the "themes" of the rest of the paper? They weren't. Or is the paper about the many treatments available to prevent the anxiety caused by agoraphobia? Yes. The paper goes on to discuss antidepressants, thought stopping, and emotive imagery and how they are used as treatments for agoraphobia. Also, you don't want to put a reference on the end of your thesis statement because that makes it appear as if you were deriving it from another source (in this case, Nydegger, 2012). So the thesis could be rewritten as: "This paper will discuss the use of antidepressants, thought stopping, and emotive imagery as treatments for the anxiety and distress caused by agoraphobia." This rewrite is clearer in terms of what the paper is about and where it is heading.

From a "D" paper on depression:
"The real key to remember when looking at the causes of depression is that there aren't any single outstanding and significant factors for it."

A few things here. First, the sentence is ungrammatical. Try reading it out loud. Second, it is too conversational - this is an APA style paper, not a blog post! Avoid contractions in scientific writing and common (or colloquial) expressions like "the real key." So is this paper about the causes of depression? Is it going to discuss the "factors" and their interplay in causing depression? The actual paper is something of a disorganized mishmash of symptoms and treatments, but the thesis could be rewritten as "This paper will discuss the symptoms of depression and their treatment through the use of selective serotonin reuptake inhibitors (SSRIs), behavior activation, and transcranial magnetic stimulation (TMS)."

From a different "F" paper on Munchausen Syndrome:
"This paper will shed some light on two aspects of this complex mental disorder including the history of the disorder and an effective treatment plan for the disorder. The paper will end by sharing what became of Julie Gregory."

This paper would best be characterized as a free-flowing literary exercise by the student - something akin to "What I find interesting about Munchausen syndrome." The thesis statement attempts to provide some guidance about the future of the paper, and the last sentence is a call-back to a case study presented earlier in the introduction. It is too conversational and too general. The paper requires a lot of revision, but the thesis statement could read something like: "This paper will discuss the history, symptoms, and treatment of Munchausen Syndrome by Proxy." It's as simple as that.

A Complete Introduction: Example

No introduction is perfect, and as they say in counseling, "progress, not perfection," but below I've reproduced the introduction from an "A-" paper on the bystander effect in children:

"From a young age, children are taught about the Golden Rule: treat others the way you would want to be treated. Nevertheless, a phenomenon called the bystander effect breaks the Golden Rule. The bystander effect occurs when a person in distress receives no support, even when surrounded by a group of observers (Darley & Latane, 1968). A multitude of studies have been conducted to understand why the bystander effect occurs in humans. One factor is the diffusion of responsibility between the members of the group that witness the event (Mathas & Kahn, 1975). Another factor is an adult's desire to behave in a socially acceptable way by following the social cues of the people surrounding them (Horowitz, 1971). However, children can be prone to conform to social norms when they are involved in situations where someone needs help. This paper will examine the major social and psychological factors that contribute to the bystander effect in children and compare the results to those from adults."

The main thing that jumps out in this paragraph is that all of the references are from the 1970s. On the positive side, the student is citing the foundational work in this area (Darley & Latane, 1968), but on the other hand, all of the research is 50+ years old. Surely there has been more recent research on the bystander effect that they could note? The thesis statement could also be clearer in terms of the "social and psychological factors" that contribute to the bystander effect. Although the student writes about the diffusion of responsibility and social cues in the paragraph, they are not included in the thesis statement. Again though, the writing does not have to be perfect in order to be clear, and this is a good introduction.

The Body

Once you have your thesis statement, the rest of your paper writes itself. Well, almost. The body of your paper, to go back to the hourglass analogy, is where your paper gets specific and you talk about individual research studies. How much should you talk about each study? Well, here the APA style manual becomes oddly specific. While discouraging single-sentence paragraphs, the ideal is to write paragraphs of three to five sentences without going over one typed page. The APA refers to this as the ideal "unit length," and I would agree - split up your paragraphs based on what you said the paper would be about in your thesis statement.

But how do you get to that point? Your thesis statement is going to be derived from the research articles you have collected for your paper. I tell students to try to identify three "themes" or "topics" or "commonalities" to use in their paper, which will be reflected in the thesis statement. The "themes" will vary from paper to paper based on the topic you choose and the research which is available, but there are a number of common themes which work across all papers. For example, many conditions have multiple treatments which are available, so you might examine each of these in a different paragraph. This is effective in that it also allows you to "compare and contrast" the different treatments. Again, the paper writes itself.

Many topics in clinical psychology can follow a "definition, causes, symptoms, and treatments" format. So whether you are writing about agoraphobia, body dysmorphic disorder, obsessive-compulsive disorder (OCD), or trichotillomania (TTM), you can have a paragraph which defines the disorder, followed by one which discusses the causes (if they are known, but this can be speculation too), followed by a paragraph on the symptoms, and then one on the treatment (or treatments) available. A few things about this structure though. Defining the phenomena that your paper is about does not mean to write something like "*Webster's* defines _____ as _____" because you are no longer a child in grade school. Find a research article that defines the issue, and DO NOT use a dictionary, Wikipedia, or an encyclopedia as your source for the definition. Causes and symptoms can often be combined into one paragraph, and if you find multiple treatments for your topic, each of them can be a seperate paragraph in your paper.

Topics in cognitive or social psychology are less likely to involve "treatments," but they are in some ways easier topics for extracting "themes" from the research. For example, if you choose context-dependent memory for your topic, the themes which emerge can be as simple as one paragraph defining what is means, a second paragraph on the conditions under which it operates, and a third paragraph on how it fits into our understanding of how memory works. Similarly, if you are interested in a topic in social psychology, you might be interested in the topic of attitudes - what they are (definition), how they develop, and how they change. Easy peasy!

The number of topics you could choose in psychology is pretty much infinite, and so the number of "themes" is even "more infinite" (if such a thing is possible). Oftentimes the themes which you identify will be something subject specific, such as comparison of different approaches to the same topic (like treatments of depression or OCD), or ways of measuring the topic of interest (like in autism spectrum disorder or Alzheimer's research). Don't be afraid to go where the research takes you - the "themes" discussed above are just ones which are the easiest to identify.

Ideally, you will be able to find multiple sources to include in each paragraph. From a professor's standpoint, it makes for dull reading when a paper reads like "here's a paragraph on this study, and now here's another paragraph on a second study that shows something else, and then here's a third paragraph about a third study I read." To be fair, that structure represents the majority of "B" and "C" papers that I read (but more of that later in the book). The ability to integrate different research articles into the same paragraph shows a high level of understanding of the material, and that will undoubtedly be reflected in the grade on the paper.

With all of that said, let us now dive into the body of three different student papers on three different topics!

From an "A" paper on seasonal affective disorder (SAD):

"Murray et al. (2005) theorized that effective treatment is concurrent with circadian phase advancement, or that the body's natural cycles affect SAD. They conducted a blind study of 78 outpatients where one group received a placebo pill and LT, and the other group received the opposite. They compared the administration of Fluoxetine and light treatment, finding that both treatments were successful. However, most importantly, the study showed that the degree of phase change did not correlate with the level of symptom improvement. In other words, the alteration of the patients' circadian rhythms from the norm does not cause SAD. Antidepressant medication has been proven to be an effective and perhaps an even simpler treatment method in comparison to the other, more complicated treatment options (LT or cognitive behavioral counseling). Antidepressant medication has the lowest remission rate among all treatment methods, at around 41% (Roecklein, 2012). Therefore, while the administration of antidepressant medication may be an effective treatment for SAD, it is not the most optimal for increasing remission."

One of the reasons why this is an "A" paragraph is that it integrates multiple sources (the Murray et al., 2005, and the Roecklein, 2012) on the same "theme." It also specifically and effectively describes how a study was done ("blind study of 78 outpatients"), who the participants were, what the manipulations were, and how the results turned out. Further, the student provides a summary of the results ("in other words, the alteration . . .") which eliminates a possible cause of SAD, while putting it in the context of other treatments of the same condition - antidepressants vs. LT vs. cognitive behavioral counseling. The student then integrates a second study to show that antidepressants are effective while also being suboptimal. The paragraph is well-written and shows that the student understands the issues in SAD research, including alternative treatments. Nicely done!

From a "C" paper on Alzheimer's Disease (AD):
"Every patient diagnosed with AD transitions through predictable decline. It begins with forgetfulness and terminates with the inability to speak or walk (Barinaga, 1998). Yet, in most cases, behavioral therapy helps patients to remember basic functions. Therapy can help stop them from screaming, biting, and hitting (Barinaga, 1998). Before, when patients were treated with antipsychotic drugs and physical restraint, it clouded their minds and increased agitation. With behavioral aids, such as depicting a process that the patient should mimic, 50% of patients improved 1-3 points on a 1-8 point scale. Afterward, they were able to dress themselves alone or with minimal help. In fact, in a study of 2400 affected person Franssen identified infantile reflexes as the disease worsens that result in muscle stiffness, or paratonia. To caretakers, this is often misconstrued as resistance but in actuality is simple inability of the muscles (Barinaga, 1998)."

There is improper citation throughout this paragraph, but at least the student is trying. What is the 1-8 point scale that the patients are improving 1-3 points on? What year did Franssen complete the research on infantile reflexes? So many questions, and since this is often an issue for students, citation and reference are covered in more detail in the next section of this book. The student does a good job of trying to integrate multiple studies into the same paragraph on the predictable decline seen in AD, but clarity is an issue. They start a sentence with the word "before." Before what? Before the study? Earlier in the paper? Before current treatment methods? The term is ambiguous. A further issue is in the citation of the Barinaga (1998) study. If you are going to spend an entire paragraph discussing the same study, it is better to rewrite the second sentence to "Barinaga (1998) writes that AD begins with forgetfulness and terminates with the inability to speak or walk." This structure eliminates the need to keep citing the same study parenthetically throughout the paragraph (in this case, three times) as long as they are discussing the same study (meaning the Barinaga study).

From an "F" paper on bystander intervention:
"In addition, situational ambiguity adds another factor to the bystander effect. Situation ambiguity can be defined as being ignorant to the matter at hand. For example, if a person sees a guy and girl play fighting. One may assume that it is a domestic altercation and that they need to intervene, yet it is the total opposite. People do not want to involve themselves especially when what they thought they've seen is really not what they saw. Another example could be if one sees a young guy on the side of the street lying on the ground puking, one could assume he is drunk and probably on some type of drug. The case is that the guy is seriously ill from a rare disease, yet no one stops and checks on him. In addition, If a person is dressed in a certain way, one may be less likely to help them and vice versa. 'People attribute what they see to helping others in most situations where help is needed' (Fischer, 2013)."

Although the citation at the end of the paragraph is better than nothing, it follows several sentences of conversational non sequiturs. For the record, always avoid using the term "puking" in your academic writing. Could this paragraph be salvaged? Of course it could. Basically, it's about how situational ambiguity impacts the bystander effect. The definition of it should be followed by a citation, and the examples should not be about "play fighting" and "puking," although to be fair, the student is making an effort to generate original examples. Citations should occur throughout the paragraph. This would allow the paper to read more like an academic paper than a stream-of-consciousness experiment. Obviously, the paragraph is also written in a style that is best characterized as "conversational" but perhaps more accurately as "vernacular." Try to remember that you're not telling your friends about the bystander intervention, you're writing an academic paper for your professor.

Conclusion

The final paragraph of your paper, logically enough, is the conclusion. What goes into the conclusion? Remembering our hourglass analogy, the paper ends by broadening the discussion - mentioning future research and how the topic is related to the future of humanity or otherwise improves the human condition.

Some students begin the conclusion with a restatement of the thesis, but this is not really necessary. In the sense of writing to a formula, it's fine, but you are likely to be looking for ways to edit your paper down, and so a restatement of the thesis is an easy thing to cut. So include a restatement or don't, depending on the length of your paper. I mention this because in my own academic career, editing is a huge issue, and I have never had an editor ask me to "write more" on a particular topic. Space in research journals is limited, and so they want to cut articles down as much as they can in order to publish as many articles as possible. I had an experience early in my academic career where I sent a 35-page article to a journal. They liked it, but requested that I cut it down to fifteen pages. Fifteen! I cut the paper to 17 pages and resubmitted it, saying that I couldn't find any more places to cut. They said "ok" and published it. The point is that editing for length is important and always something to keep in mind.

An ideal thing to discuss in the conclusion are future areas of research, because nothing shows greater insight than making intelligent suggestions about where you see future research on a particular topic heading. Suggestions for future research are also a subtle way to insert your own thoughts and opinions about the research into your paper. I always tell my students to avoid "I" statements (like "I believe") or "in my opinion" because researchers never use these phrases in their own writing. Research topics are supposed to be about "science" and so there is no room for "beliefs" or opinions. But as a rational, educated, thinking adult who has reviewed the literature on a particular topic, of course you have some informed opinions about the research and where you believe it should go next. YOUR perspective on a field is invaluable, but it has to be phrased in the proper way.

Another thing to keep in mind is that the articles you are reading also present their own ideas about future research. After all, the researchers believe that their work is valuable and the topic is in need of further study too! Like everywhere else in your paper, if "your" ideas about future research are actually someone else's ideas, be sure to give them proper citation.

From an "A" paper on Cognitive Behavioral Therapy:
"In conclusion, this paper has examined CBT and how variations on it are used to benefit patients with anxiety disorders. Further research for I/EP CBT should determine which groups of patients should receive emotional processing and interpersonal problems based on the patients' degree of those problems. New research on NET and CLIN CBT should include a placebo control group in order to produce more reliable results. Also, subsequent research of the therapeutic relationship can better distinguish whether positive results of therapy determine better therapeutic relationships or vice versa. As advances are made in all of this research, many people with anxiety disorders will benefit from a better therapy experience and fewer anxiety symptoms."

I freely admit that this sample is a bit difficult to understand because it is full of acronyms and taken out of context; however, it does a number of things well. First, it "restates the thesis" without literally restating the thesis. The suggestions for future research allow the student to provide a subtle critique of the studies they have read by suggesting different manipulations as a reliability check. And it finishes broadly with a statement about how through further research, therapy can be more effective and people can experience fewer symptoms of anxiety. A brighter future awaits! Well done.

From a "C+" paper on lithium as a treatment for Bipolar Disorder:
"In conclusion, despite the negative connotations associated with lithium, it is still the leading drug for treatment of Bipolar Disorder, with the highest proven effectiveness and the most research done. While it is ineffective at treating depressive episodes, lithium continues to be proven to be useful at drastically improving the quality of life for those suffering with bipolar disorder. However, research should continue to be done regarding lithium and other possible health benefits and risks associated with the drug."

The problem here is how noncommittal and broadly generic the writing is. Suggestions for future research need to be more specific than "other possible health benefits and risks" from the use of lithium. That suggestion "suggests" that the writer really has no idea where future research should go. On the positive side, the first sentence is a good restatement of the thesis and the research associated with lithium and its use as a treatment for bipolar disorder.

From an "F" paper on phobias:
"After looking at this research, exposure and response prevention seems to be the best choice. Contextual therapy would not be the best choice because the patient will only have a high chance of overcoming his/her phobia if they understand it and not all patients will be able to do that. Cognitive therapy is only best used in an individual treatment setting rather than in a group setting and is only ahead in this setting by 8%. If you use ERP, only 25% will possibly not respond to it, partly because of non-adherence."

I believe that when you read enough "F" papers you can see how conversational they are - like the student dictated them, the computer's voice recognition software did the best it could, and the student then handed in the paper without revising, editing, or oftentimes even bothering to read it. Granted, all of these paper sections are taken out of context, but what does it mean that cognitive therapy is "only ahead in this setting by 8%?" Is cognitive therapy in a race? And why is it that "exposure and response prevention seems to be the best choice?" Does that conclusion come from "looking at this research?" Finally, the paper doesn't end broadly, but on the word "non-adherence." Again, it is both too specific and too conversational. The raw material for a good conclusion is here though - plenty of statistics and opinions on treatment options - it is the execution of the writing that is the problem.

References

I am putting an entire section on citation and references in the next section of this book because of the problems they tend to cause for students, but since your paper will end with the references, let's talk a bit about them now too. One of the key things professors look for is that your reference page matches the citations you used in your paper. When they don't match, it's a red flag that you either don't know what you're doing or that you are plagiarizing from a different source. Both of those are bad outcomes, so be sure that the references at the end of your paper reflect the citations throughout your paper.

Another suggestion I would make is to have a "rough" reference page in progress as you are writing your paper. Since you already know what sources you are going to use for your paper when you start writing, it doesn't require much effort to create a rough mock-up of what your references will look like. This includes alphabetization! I can't count the number of papers I have received from students who didn't understand that the references are to be placed in alphabetical order. So in the same way that you are writing a rough draft of your paper, create a rough draft of your references. This allows you to avoid the pitfalls of forgetting to include a source or not properly alphabetizing them. You can always add or remove a source in your final draft, and that is also the time to be sure that your reference page is done properly.

I am also going to put a special section in here on reference alphabetization because I get a number of questions from students about it, and it can be very confusing.

Reference alphabetization

Many students have questions about what to do when different authors have the same last name (like Brown), similar last names (like Brown, Browne, and Browning), or no name at all. How is it all alphabetized in the references? Thankfully, it is not very difficult as long as you follow a few rules.

First, if a work has no author or editor, it should be alphabetized by the first important word of the title. In the examples below, the book *A Brown Pelican Marks the Spot* is alphabetized by the word "Brown" rather than "A" because "Brown" is the first meaningful word in the title.

In situations where multiple authors have the same last name, alphabetize by their first name. In the example below, Amanda Brown (with her fictional book about Taylor Swift) comes before Dan Brown (with his actual best-sellers).

What about situations where different authors have similar names, like Brown, Browne, and Browning? In cases like this, *nothing precedes something*, so an author named "Brown" would go before one named "Browne," and both would go before "Browning."

Two more notes about the mini-reference list below. Dan Brown has three books on the list, and so the book that was published earliest (*Digital Fortress*) goes before the book that was published more recently (*Angels & Demons*) even though the "D" in "Digital" comes after the "A" in "Angels" in the alphabet. Therefore, the publication date is more important than title alphabetization (which is irrelevant) when putting an author's books in a reference list. Also, the book *A Brown Pelican Marks the Spot* appears before Jackson Browne's book because, as mentioned earlier, nothing precedes something.

It is hard to imagine a research paper that would contain these particular sources (several of which I've invented), but it would be correctly alphabetized like this:

Brown, A. (2018). *Taylor Swift: A Study in Genius*. Boston, MA: Way Back Bay Books.
Brown, D. (1998). *Digital Fortress*. New York, NY: St. Martin's Press.
Brown, D. (2000). *Angels & Demons*. New York, NY: Pocket Books.
Brown, D. (2003). *The Da Vinci Code*. New York, NY: Doubleday.
A Brown Pelican Marks the Spot. (2012). Denver, CO: Rocky Mountain High Press.
Browne, J. (1999). *Still Running on Empty*. Cleveland, OH: Rock Publishing.
Browning, E. B. (2007). *Sonnets from the Portuguese: A Celebration of Love*.
    New York, NY: St. Martin's Press.
Brownwood Sports Legends. (2010). Greentop, MO: Greentop Academic Press.

Section 3 - Citations

Citations and references get their own sections because of the many problems they cause for students. It seems easy enough - you should use a citation in your paper whenever you are paraphrasing, discussing someone else's ideas, or taking a direct quote from another manuscript. But then things get complicated! Consider the following:

Here are a few questions to ask:
1. Are you making the citation "in-text" (which means as a part of your sentence) or "parenthetically" (meaning obviously, in parentheses)?
2. How often should you make a citation?
3. Is this the first time you cite the source or a subsequent time? How many authors are there, and how does that change the first time you cite the source compared to subsequent citations?
4. What if there are multiple sources within the same citation? Or there is no author for a source? What about special cases?
5. How would you cite a direct quote? And what if you needed to cite something that someone else had cited?

I wish I could say that the answers to these questions are simple and straightforward, but I also wish that I could wish for more wishes! Putting that aside, the purpose of this section will be to show you how sources are properly cited, and how this relates to the reference section of your paper.

1. Types of citation - "in-text" vs. "parenthetical"

An in-text citation includes the authors' names as a part of the sentence, so an example would look something like this (from an "A" paper on eyewitness testimony):

"Valentine and Maras (2011) performed an experiment to determine the effect of cross-examination on the accuracy of the eyewitness."

A parenthetical citation of the same sentence (rewritten) would look like:

"An experiment was performed to determine the effect of cross-examination on the accuracy of the eyewitness (Valentine & Maras, 2011)."

So which way is better? It depends, and this gets into issues of active vs. passive voice, and everything else you've forgotten from your high school English classes. In general, active voice is preferred in academic writing, but what does that mean?

With the active voice, the subject of the sentence is performing the action, as in: "Valentine and Maras (2011) performed an experiment . . . "

Using the passive voice to state the same thing with an in-text citation would be "An experiment was performed by Valentine and Maras (2011) to determine . . ." or if you wanted to write it as a parenthetical citation, it would look like the previous example "An experiment was performed to determine the effect of cross-examination on the accuracy of the eyewitness (Valentine & Maras, 2011)."

About the same number of words in either case, but the passive voice puts the subject ("Valentine and Maras") after the verb ("performed"), making the sentence less clear. A non-academic example makes this distinction even more obvious: "I ate my dinner at 6 PM today" (active) "Today at 6 PM, my dinner was eaten by me" (passive). Sounds ridiculous right? What if a whole paper was written like that? So, be aware of the distinction between active and passive voice in your writing, and try to use the active voice when possible.

2. How often should you make a citation?

I have had a number of students over the years believe that they could write an entire paragraph and by sticking a citation at the end, everything would be ok. This is not so! This is a question of how often citation should occur, and the answer, as much in life, is "it depends." For example, if you cite an article in-text, and continue to discuss the same article throughout the paragraph, there is no need to keep citing it because it is obvious which article you are discussing. Here is an example from an unpublished article I wrote on odors and memory:

"In their review of odor perception and mnemonic theory, Stevenson and Boakes (2003) briefly discussed the usage of odor as a contextual cue in incidental associations. While they theorized that effortful associations are required to form long-term memory traces, incorporating incidental contextual cues may achieve the same effect. Therefore, memory for odors is not different from memory for stimuli in other modalities."

The following is an example of the exact same paragraph, but with a parenthetical citation in the first sentence, which makes an in-text citation necessary in the next sentence (otherwise, it would be unclear who the "they" was referring to). While this is less than ideal (to me, it reads like the same article is actually two different articles), it at least makes sense as to who was doing the research:

"In their review of odor perception and mnemonic theory, the researchers (Stevenson & Boakes, 2003) briefly discussed the usage of odor as a contextual cue in incidental associations. While Stevenson and Boakes (2003) theorized that effortful associations are required to form long-term memory traces, incorporating incidental contextual cues may achieve the same effect. Therefore, memory for odors is not different from memory for stimuli in other modalities."

However, this is the form I often see in student papers, and it is a good example of an inappropriate method of citation:

"In their review of odor perception and mnemonic theory, the researchers briefly discussed the usage of odor as a contextual cue in incidental associations. While they theorized that effortful associations are required to form long-term memory traces, incorporating incidental contextual cues may achieve the same effect. Therefore, memory for odors is not different from memory for stimuli in other modalities (Stevenson & Boakes, 2003)."

Is the parenthetical citation of Stevenson and Boakes referring to everything in the previous paragraph? Or is it just referring to the last sentence? It's unclear. I believe that students make the assumption that the citation at the end of the paragraph implicitly covers everything that came before, but when you have multiple sources discussed within the same paragraph, it's impossible for the reader to determine what information came from which source. So just don't do it - don't write an entire paragraph and then stick a citation at the end.

Here is a paragraph from an "A" student paper on conformity that illustrates in-text and parenthetical citations with multiple sources, which I have also included in a reference list so you can see what that would look like:

"Gender is another predictor of conformity that has been documented by researchers. A meta-analysis of 148 studies was conducted by Eagly and Carli (1981) to see if men and women differ in how easily they are influenced. Surveillance and non-surveillance group pressure situations were looked at, and women were found to be more conforming than men. One study, conducted by Santee and Jackson (1982) tried to answer the question of why this difference exists by looking at how men and women judge conformity. They had 133 undergraduate participants observe a simulation of a conformity situation. The simulations had five levels of conformity. After observing one of the simulations, participants made normative and attributional judgments. An additional 40 undergraduate student participants viewed these simulations and gave responses to give the "best possible impression." This study found that females consider conformity to be a more positive behavior than males. Females are expected to be more sensitive than males, so they conform to keep peace. Males interpret deviating from a group as enhancing self image, since nonconforming behavior attracts attention (Eagly, 1987). Another example of this gender difference in conformity data is provided by Maslach, Santee, and Wade (1987). They state that gender roles are responsible for the likelihood of conformity in males and females. A part of the masculine gender role is to be independent and self-confident. The authors stated that a part of the feminine role is to be sensitive to others, so conformity is a way of promoting harmony in social situations. These personality traits are attributed to each gender and are the basis of their conforming or nonconforming behavior."

Eagly, A. H. (1987). *Sex differences in social behavior: A social role interpretation.* Hillsdale, NJ: Erlbaum.

Eagly, A. H., & Carli, L. L. (1981). Sex of researchers and sex-typed communications as determinants of sex differences in influenceability: A meta-analysis of social influence studies. *Psychological Bulletin, 90*(1), 1-20. doi:10.1037/0033-2909.90.1.1

Maslach, C., Santee, R. T., & Wade, C. (1987). Individuation, gender role, and dissent: Personality mediators of situational forces. *Journal of Personality and Social Psychology, 53* (6), 1088-1093. doi:10.1037/0022-3514.53.6.1088

Santee, R. T., & Jackson, S. E. (1982). Identity implications of conformity: Sex differences in normative and attributional judgments. *Social Psychology Quarterly, 45*(2), 121-125.

Although I believe this paragraph makes too much use of the passive voice ("One study, conducted by," "data is provided by"), it does an outstanding job of integrating different types of sources (books and journal articles) into a cohesive discussion of how gender is predictive of conformity. It also allows you to see that when making an in-text citation, you don't need to keep citing the same study in every sentence as long as you don't switch the discussion to a different study.

3. Is this the first time you cite the source or a subsequent time? How many authors are there, and how does that change the first time you cite the source compared to subsequent citations?

Citation should be fairly straightforward, and much of the time it is. Basically, when a source has one or two authors, mention all of them every time you make a citation. When a source has three or more authors, things get more complicated; not impossible, but more complicated. An illustration for each possible scenario follows:

Source with one author:
When a source has one author, things are pretty straightforward - the author should be cited every time the reference is cited, whether the citation is made in-text or parenthetically. For example:

Source
Harrison, K. (2003). Television viewers' ideal body proportions: The case of the curvaceously thin woman. *Sex Roles, 48,* 255–264.

In-text format
1st citation - Harrison (2003) found that . . .
Subsequent citation - Harrison (2003) found that . . .

Parenthetical format
1st citation - however, others (Harrison, 2003) have found that . . .
Subsequent citation - however, others (Harrison, 2003) have found that . . .

Source with two authors:
When a source has two authors, things remain pretty straightforward - both should be cited each time the reference is cited, whether the citation is made in-text or parenthetically. The only real difference is that if the citation is made in-text, be sure to use "and" between the authors names, and if the citation is made parenthetically, you use an ampersand ("&") between the authors names. For example:

Source
McDaniel, M. A., & Einstein, G. O. (2007). *Prospective memory : An overview and synthesis of an emerging field.* Thousand Oaks, CA: SAGE Publications.

In-text format
1st citation - McDaniel and Einstein (2007) found that . . .
Subsequent citation - McDaniel and Einstein (2007) found that . . .

Parenthetical format
1st citation - however, others (McDaniel & Einstein, 2007) have found that . . .
Subsequent citation - however, others (McDaniel & Einstein, 2007) have found that . . .

Source with three, four, or five authors:
When a source has three, four, or five authors, things get a little more complicated. All of their names should be cited the first time the reference is cited, but subsequent citations should just be the last name of the first author followed by "et al." (which means "and others").

As when there were only two authors, if the citation is made in-text, be sure to use "and" between the authors' names, and if the citation is made parenthetically, you use an ampersand ("&") between the authors' names.

Also, it should be noted that in lists of three or more items (like three or more author names), APA style requires the use of an Oxford or "serial" comma. Practically speaking, in this context, this means that a comma goes before the "and" or "&" and the name of the last author in a series. So for example, if you had three authors (Gurney, Pine, & Wiseman, 2013), it would be appropriate to write in a first citation "Gurney, Pine, and Wiseman (2013)" and inappropriate to write "Gurney, Pine and Wiseman (2013)." The first example correctly puts a comma after "Pine" where the second example does not. It makes even more sense if you look at the many examples below.

It is going to be a bit redundant, but I will give examples of three, four, and five author source citations:

Source with three authors:

Source
Krähenbühl, S., Blades, M., & Eiser, C. (2009). The effect of repeated questioning on children's accuracy and consistency in eyewitness testimony. *Legal and Criminological Psychology, 14*(2), 263-278. doi:10.1348/135532508X398549

In-text format
1st citation - Krähenbühl, Blades, and Eiser (2009) found that . . .
Subsequent citation - Krähenbühl et al. (2009) found that . . .

Parenthetical format
1st citation - however, others (Krähenbühl, Blades, & Eiser, 2009) have found that . . .
Subsequent citation - however, others (Krähenbühl et al., 2009) have found that . . .

Source with four authors:

Source
Eich, T. S., Murayama, K., Castel, A. D., & Knowlton, B. J. (2014). The dynamic effects of age-related stereotype threat on explicit and implicit memory performance in older adults. *Social Cognition, 32*(6), 559-570. doi: 10.1521/soco.2014.32.6.559

In-text format
1st citation - Eich, Murayama, Castel, and Knowlton (2014) found that . . .
Subsequent citation - Eich et al. (2014) found that . . .

Parenthetical format
1st citation - however, others (Eich, Murayama, Castel, & Knowlton, 2014) have found that . . .
Subsequent citation - however, others (Eich et al., 2014) have found that . . .

Source with five authors:

Source
Benedetti, F., Mayberg, H. S., Wager, T. D., Stohler, C. S., & Zubieta, J. (2005). Neurobiological mechanisms of the placebo effect. *The Journal of Neuroscience, 25*(45), 10390-10402.

In-text format
1st citation - Benedetti, Mayberg, Wager, Stohler, and Zubieta (2005) found that . . .
Subsequent citation - Benedetti et al. (2005) found that . . .

Parenthetical format
1st citation - however, others (Benedetti, Mayberg, Wager, Stohler, and Zubieta, 2005) have found that . . .
Subsequent citation - however, others (Benedetti et al., 2005) have found that . . .

Source with six or more authors:
In some ways, things get simpler when a manuscript has six or more authors, because you just need to cite the last name of the first author followed by "et al." (which means, again, "and others") whenever the work appears in the text. For example, if a manuscript were to have more than seven authors, the "six author +" format would look like:

Source
Cortese, S., Holtmann, M., Banaschewski, T., Buitelaar, J., Coghill, D., Danckaerts, M.,
   . . . Sergeant, J. (2013). Practitioner review: Current best practice in the
   management of adverse events during treatment with ADHD medications in
   children and adolescents. *Journal of Child Psychology & Psychiatry, 54*(3),
   227-246. doi:10.1111/jcpp.12036

In-text format
1st citation - Cortese et al. (2013) found that . . .
Subsequent citation - Cortese et al. (2013) found that . . .

Parenthetical format
1st citation - however, others (Cortese et al., 2013) have found that . . .
Subsequent citation - however, others (Cortese et al., 2013) have found that . . .

4. What if there are multiple sources within the same citation? Or there is no author for a source? What about special cases?

This is pretty much an "everything else" kind of question, and the examples are not all that likely to come up in student papers, but it's good to be prepared. It should also be noted that each of the following scenarios involve parenthetical citations, as in-text citation would not apply. So, under the following scenarios, here is what you would do!

Multiple sources from the same author (or authors) from the same year:
If you cite multiple manuscripts from the same author (or authors) from the same year, differentiate between the works by placing lowercase letters (a, b, c) after the year in BOTH the citation and the references. This makes it clear which article you are citing throughout your paper. For example, Daniel Kahneman is a famous Nobel Prize winning psychologist (in Economics in 2002) who has published a lot during his career, so it would not be surprising to use two of his works from the same year. Remember to separate the two sources within the parentheses with a semicolon. The rules for parenthetical first and

subsequent citation remain the same, based on the the number of authors of the source. For example:

Sources
Kahneman, D. (2003a). A psychological perspective on economics. *American Economic Review, 93*, 162-168.
Kahneman, D. (2003b). A perspective on judgment and choice: Mapping bounded rationality. *American Psychologist, 58*, 697-720.

Parenthetical format
1st citation - however, others (Kahneman, 2003a; Kahneman, 2003b) have found that . . .
Subsequent citation - however, others (Kahneman, 2003a; Kahneman, 2003b) have found that. . .

Multiple sources from the same author (or authors) from different years:
If you cite multiple manuscripts from the same author (or authors) from different years, arrange them by year, with "in press" citations placed last. Continuing with the Kahneman examples, here are two journal articles and a chapter in an edited book:

Sources
Kahneman, D. (1991). Judgment and decision making: A personal view. *Psychological Science, 2*, 142-145.
Kahneman, D. (1994). New challenges to the rationality assumption. *Journal of Institutional and Theoretical Economics, 150*, 18-36.
Kahneman, D. (2000). Evaluation by moments: Past and future. In D. Kahneman & A Tversky (Eds.), *Choices, values, and frames* (pp. 693-708). New York, NY: Cambridge University Press and the Russell Sage Foundation.

Parenthetical format
1st citation - however, others (Kahneman, 1991, 1994, 2000) have found that . . .
Subsequent citation - however, others (Kahneman, 1991, 1994, 2000) have found that . . .

Multiple sources within the same set of parentheses:
Whenever you cite two or more sources within the same set of parentheses, they should be in alphabetical order and separated by semicolons. The order is not based on the year of publication, the importance of the work, or the prominence of the researchers, but literally on the alphabetical order of the names. For example, Daniel Kahneman collaborated for years on research with fellow psychologist Amos Tversky (they became friends after arguing with each other about whether people are good intuitive statisticians) and so here is how some of their research would be presented:

Sources:
Kahneman, D., & Deaton, A. (2010). High income improves evaluation of life but not emotional well-being. *Proceedings of the National Academy of Sciences of the United States of America, 107*(38), 16489-16493.
Tversky, A., Slovic, P., & Kahneman, D. (1990). The causes of preference reversal. *American Economic Review, 80*, 204-217.

Parenthetical format
1st citation - however, others (Kahneman & Deaton, 2010; Tversky, Slovic, & Kahneman, 1990) have found that . . .
Subsequent citation - however, others (Kahneman & Deaton, 2010; Tversky et al., 1990) have found that . . .

Since the "K" in Kahneman comes before the "T" in Tversky in the alphabet, it also comes first in the parenthetical citation. Please also note that the Tversky citation changes to "Tversky et al., 1990" in the subsequent citation because the rules dealing with citations with three or more authors are still applicable.

Let's just throw one more source into the mix, also from 2010 and also with Kahneman as an author, to make this even more clear:

Source:
Frederick, S., Kahneman, D., & Mochon, D. (2010). Elaborating a simpler theory of anchoring. *Journal of Consumer Psychology, 20*(1), 17-19.

Parenthetical format
1st citation - however, others (Frederick, Kahneman, & Mochon, 2010; Kahneman & Deaton, 2010; Tversky, Slovic, & Kahneman, 1990) have found that . . .
Subsequent citation - however, others (Frederick et al., 2010; Kahneman & Deaton, 2010; Tversky et al., 1990) have found that . . .

Again, the "F" in Frederick comes before the "K" in Kahneman and the "T" in Tversky, and the subsequent citation also changes with the number of authors.

Sources with no identifiable author:
I have never seen an article in a research journal without an author, so this is going to be a vanishingly rare occurrence in a student paper; however, we should discuss it because it is relevant to material you use from the web, which may or may not have an identifiable author. It's also relevant to historical works like *Beowulf*, and perhaps *Beowulf* is somehow related to your paper, and who knows who wrote *Beowulf*?

For example, perhaps you are doing a paper on violence and wanted to include an update on the school shooting at Sandy Hook in 2012. If the web page had no identifiable author, then just cite the first few words of the title of the source (in quotation marks) and the year it was published. Also, like the other "special cases" in this section on citation, it should be noted that this applies to parenthetical citations, as in-text citation would not really be appropriate. For example:

Source
A look back: Sandy Hook Elementary School shooting (2018, June 7). Retrieved from http://www.cbsnews.com/pictures/a-look-back-sandy-hook-elementary-school-shooting

Parenthetical format
1st citation - ... in the aftermath of school shootings ("A look back: Sandy Hook," 2018).
Subsequent citation - ... in the aftermath of school shootings ("A look back: Sandy Hook," 2018).

To go back to the *Beowulf* example, here is how it would be cited and referenced:

Source
Beowulf. (1992). Translated by R.K. Gordon. Mineola, NY: Dover Publications.

Parenthetical format
1st citation - Violence in the media has a long history (*Beowulf*, 1992) and ...
Subsequent citation - Violence in the media has a long history (*Beowulf*, 1992) and ...

In the unlikely circumstance that "Anonymous" is listed as the author, cite that (and the year of publication). The only example of this that I can think of was a book from the 1990s about Bill Clinton's run for the presidency in 1992 called *Primary Colors*. The book's author was "Anonymous" and there was quite a bit of speculation at the time over who wrote the book, since it had a lot of "insider" knowledge about the campaign. It turned out to be written by political columnist Joe Klein. So if you wanted to use that source in your paper (perhaps on the topic of political psychology) it would look like:

Source
Anonymous. (1996). *Primary colors: A novel of politics*. New York, NY: Random House.

Parenthetical format
1st citation - Books about campaigns have a long history (Anonymous, 1996) and ...
Subsequent citation - Books about campaigns have a long history (Anonymous, 1996) and ...

5. How would you cite a direct quote? And what if you needed to cite something that someone else had cited?

Sometimes we need to use a direct quote in a paper in order to get the wording exactly right; however, I strongly discourage students from using direct quotes very frequently. Like block quotes (to be discussed momentarily), direct quotes can be used to pad out the length of a paper, and that can be pretty obvious to a professor. Some papers

I've read are really just strings of direct quotes bound together with some intervening explanatory sentences. There have also been a number of times I've scratched my head and asked, "Why did they need to take a direct quote of THAT?!" Nothing shows an inability to paraphrase like the overuse of direct quotes. Well, plagiarism shows the same inability, but that's a topic for later.

Block quotes are to be assiduously avoided in a paper for the simple reason that everyone in academia knows why they are used - to stretch out a paper for students who just couldn't make it to the minimum page limit. As I mentioned earlier, you will be requested to "edit down" your paper in revision, not add more! So I'm not even going to give an example of a "student paper" block quote because I've never seen it done appropriately.

Direct quotes

Whenever you use a direct quote from one of your sources, be sure to always specify an author, year, and page (or paragraph, in the case of websites and some other media) in the citation of the quotation. Direct quotations are only appropriate if they are 40 words or less. If they're more than 40 words, they should be incorporated into a block quotation (and indented ½ inch from the left margin), but I've already said that you should avoid block quotations, so just be sure your direct quotes are less than 40 words!

A direct quotation must faithfully reproduce the spelling, wording, and punctuation of the original source material, so you can't edit or change it. If there is a particular word (or words) that you want to emphasize within the quotation, put them into italics. Also, and I've gotten this question before, if your direct quotation contains an internal citation, what should you do? Include it in the quotation (after all, you're "faithfully reproducing" the original source), but don't add it to your reference list: you're not using it as a source, the other author is. If you're taking a direct quote from an online source that doesn't have page numbers (and not many do), use the paragraph number that the quote appears in, and use the abbreviation "para" in your citation. For convenience, I've included an example of this below in the "as cited in" section.

With that said, let's look at some examples from student papers:

From an "A" paper on SAD:

Source
Roecklein, K. A., Schumacher, J. A., Miller, M. A., & Ernecoff, N. C. (2012). Cognitive
 and behavioral predictors of light therapy use. *PLoS ONE, 7*(6), e39275. doi:
 10.371/journal.pone.0039275

Roecklein et al. (2012) states that "treatments that impact social support and self-efficacy improve treatment response" (p. 1), allowing for lower remission rates.

Almost everything about this is good. They use the appropriate "subsequent citation" form for the Roecklein, Schumacher, Miller, and Ernecoff (2012) source, and then put the page number in parentheses after the direct quotation. It's unclear to me what the relationship between the page number listed in the citation ("1") and the page number listed in the reference ("e39275") is, but this is an "A" paper, and not a perfect paper. The use of the direct quotation is also appropriate because it would be difficult to paraphrase without using the exact same words. Finally, the student was able to incorporate the direct quotation into the sentence without "making" it the sentence. Good work!

From a "C-" paper on conformity:

Source
Lazarus, R. S. (1991). *Emotion and adaptation.* New York, NY: Oxford University Press.

"Happiness is elicited by events that an individual perceives as goal congruent" (Lazarus, 1991).

A very common mistake that students make is to have the entire sentence be a direct quotation, and this student's paper is full of examples of that. Give a direct quotation, and then talk about it. Then do it again. And again. Does this sentence REALLY need to be a direct quotation? Is it providing information that can't be paraphrased by the student? The student correctly cites the Lazarus book and also includes the year, but fails to include the page number where the quotation appeared. Using the same structure as the "A" paper above, and making up a page number for the quotation (since I don't have the source), a rewrite of the sentence would look like: "Lazarus (1991) believes that happiness comes from 'events that an individual perceives as goal congruent' (p.231) in the context of their lives."

From an "F" paper on bystander intervention:

Source
   Aronson, Elliot, Timothy D. Wilson, and Robyn M. Akert.(2005). Social Psychology. Upper Saddle River, NJ: Prentice Hall. 162-64. Print.

Diffused responsibility is "The phenomenon whereby each bystander's sense of responsibility to help decreases as the number of witnesses increases" (Aronson, 364).

Let's begin by discussing the source the student chose to use. It's a textbook! As a tertiary source, it's not appropriate. The way they wrote the reference is reproduced verbatim too, and it's a mishmash of errors and mistakes. Let's start with the indentation, which is backwards and doesn't include a "hanging indent." The author names are sometimes presented "last name first" and sometimes as "last name last." The student also chose to include the authors' first names in the reference. Spacing is a minor issue, but they also chose to include the page numbers they used in the reference (which you don't need to do with a book) and interestingly, the page range in the reference doesn't match the page number listed in the citation. That's curious! They also included "Print." at the end of the reference, which is superfluous.

As to the direct quote itself, it's too long, and the words "The phenomenon whereby" are unnecessary. Within the citation they include only the first author of a three author textbook, and it's questionable what the "364" refers to. Is it the publication year? The page number? Let's assume it's the page number, but then they need to add the year (2005) and "p." to the citation. The sentence is best rewritten as "Diffused responsibility occurs when 'each bystander's sense of responsibility to help decreases as the number of witnesses increases' (Aronson, Wilson, & Akert, 2005, p. 364)." So again, there are no "bad papers," just papers that need to be rewritten.

As cited in

Let's imagine that you find a quote that you like from a famous author, but it's actually taken out of context in a different book? For example, I was writing a paper on odor and memory, and found a quote I liked from Rudyard Kipling in the book *Senses and Sensibility* by Jillyn Smith. But how could I use the quote without scouring all of the writings of Rudyard Kipling? Well, there's an easy solution and a more difficult solution. Let's talk about the difficult version first. If you want or need to cite a source that you have not read in the original, you can use the following format:

Rudyard Kipling once said that "Smells are surer than sights or sounds to make your heartstrings crack" (as cited in Smith, 1989, p.92).

Using "as cited in" spares you from having to read Rudyard Kipling's entire set of written works in order to find the one quotation that you want, and this form is frequently used when citing from a classical text. The Smith (1989) reference is included in your references because it is the work you have actually read. The page number is included in the citation because it is a direct quote. Here is how the Smith book looks in the references:

Smith, J. (1989). *Senses and Sensibility*. New York, NY: Wiley.

As a further note, you should always try to cite the original source, and only use "as cited in" when the original source is unavailable or impractical to obtain. Otherwise, it is easy to see how this method of citation could be abused or misunderstood. For example, students will sometimes use "as cited in" to talk about research articles that they weren't willing (or able) to find, because they read about them in another article. Just try to find the original source - it's out there!

That was the hard way. Here's the easy way: Plug the quotation you want to use into the googly-machine, and then cite the website that carries the quote. In this case, the sentence with the direct quote and the reference would look like this:

Rudyard Kipling once said that "Smells are surer than sights or sounds to make your heartstrings crack" (Kipling, n.d., para 1).

Kipling, R. (n.d.) Smells are surer than sounds. Retrieved June 12, 2018 from
http://www.azquotes.com/quotes/786525

Now let's "unpack" this citation a little. The author is Kipling, the website changes and is revised over time, so the date is listed as "n.d.," and since we are using a webpage, we include the paragraph that the direct quotation appears in. Since the quote is the only paragraph, then the paragraph number is 1, and that is abbreviated to "para 1" in the citation.

Ok, so maybe that's not the "easy way" to do it. Easier?

Section 4 - References

This section is a good follow-up to the section on citations because any sources which appear in your paper also need to appear in your references. A mismatch between your citations and references is a red flag to your professor that either you don't know what you're doing or you're plagiarizing some or all of your work. And it's not that difficult to properly reference sources! They all pretty much contain the same information (author, year, source information) and so it's usually just an issue of identifying the appropriate type of reference (periodical, book, web, etc.) and then being sure that the commas, periods, and parentheses are in the correct locations.

This section is intended to provide you with reference examples for just about every possible source that you will encounter in your research - from books to journal articles to video blog posts. Since most of your sources will (or at least "should!") be journal articles or academic books, we will start with those. I've also interspersed information on web-based sources, and put things like Twitter posts and Facebook updates in their own sections.

I mentioned earlier that I think it is a good policy to have a "rough" reference section going while you write your paper, and then making sure that the references conform with APA style guidelines after the writing is finished. Think of your references as the one part of your paper that your professor is sure to read, because they will! Why? Because it's the section where it is easiest to find mistakes! Reading papers takes a lot of effort, but ticking through your reference list is pretty easy work. So get them right and you will impress your professor! Here's a lot of examples of how to do them right:

Periodicals

Periodicals are works that come out "periodically," and so include research journals, magazines, and newspapers - you know, the types of sources you're supposed to be using in your paper. A generic example is pretty meaningless because every periodical has a different combination of authors, titles, etc., but it would look something like this, with the periods, numbers (###), italics, and everything else in its proper place:

First author last name, First author first name initial. First author middle name initial - if provided. (#### year of publication). Title of the journal article. *Name of the Periodical, ## volume number of periodical*(# issue number of periodical), ### page numbers of article. doi: 10.##########

Or more simply, in an actual example of a journal article, as follows from the generic example:

Dodd, K. (2010). Psychological and other non-pharmacological interventions in services for people with learning disabilities and dementia. *Advances in Mental Health and Learning Disabilities, 4*(1), 28-35. doi: 10.5042/amhld.2010.0056

Journal articles as references

Here is the APA style rule - when a journal article has seven or fewer authors, list all of them in the reference; when there are eight or more authors, only the first six authors should be listed on the reference page, followed by three ellipsis points (. . .), and then the name of the last author. Examples follow:

Journal article with one author:

Wollen, K. A. (2010). Alzheimer's Disease: The pros and cons of pharmaceutical, nutritional, botanical, and stimulatory therapies, with a discussion of treatment strategies from the perspective of patients and practitioners. *Alternative Medicine Review, 15*(3), 223–244.

Journal article with two authors:

Young, M. A., & Azam, O. A. (2003). Ruminative response style and the severity of seasonal affective disorder. *Cognitive Therapy & Research, 27*(2), 223-232.

Journal article with three authors:

Renshaw, K. D., Steketee, G., & Chambless, D. L. (2005). Involving family members in the treatment of OCD. *Cognitive Behaviour Therapy, 34*(3), 164-175. doi:10.1080/16506070510043732

Journal article with four authors:

Gloaguen, V., Cottraux, J., Cucherat, M., & Blackburn, I. (1998). A meta-analysis of the effects of cognitive therapy in depressed patients. *Journal of Affective Disorders, 49*(1), 59-72. doi:10.1016/S0165-0327(97)00199-7

Journal article with five authors:

Molin, J., Mellerup, E., Bolwig, T., Schieke, T., & Dam, H. (1999). The influence of climate on development of winter depression. *Journal of Affective Disorders, 37*(2-3), 151-155.

Journal article with six authors:

Mostafavi, A., Solhi, M., Mohammadi, M. R., Hamedi, M., Keshavarzi, M., & Akhondzadeh, S. (2014). Melatonin decreases Olanzapine induced metabolic side-effects in adolescents with bipolar disorder: A randomized double-blind placebo-controlled trial. *Acta Medica Iranica, 52*(10), 734-739.

Journal article with seven authors:

de Melo Coelho, F. G., Andrade, L. P., Pedroso, R. V., Santos-Galduroz, R. F., Gobbi, S., Costa, J. L. R., & Gobbi, L. T. B. (2013). Multimodal exercise intervention improves frontal cognitive functions and gait in Alzheimer's Disease: A controlled trial. *Geriatrics & Gerontology International, 13*(1), 198-203. doi: 10.1111/j.1447-0594.2012.00887.x

Journal article with eight or more authors:

Guétin, S. S., Portet, F. F., Picot, M. C., Pommié, C. C., Messaoudi, M. M., Djabelkir, L. L.,... Touchon, J. J. (2009). Effect of music therapy on anxiety and depression in patients with Alzheimer's type dementia: Randomised, controlled study. *Dementia & Geriatric Cognitive Disorders, 28*(1), 36-46. doi:10.1159/000229024

Note: About DOI numbers (those numbers at the end of some journal article references):
You may have noticed that some of the journal article references have DOI numbers, and some do not. DOI (digital object identifier) numbers have become pervasive in periodicals, but are not always assigned to every possible source. The idea behind them is that in the digital world, websites change or are taken down, and links can be altered or changed by whoever administers a website at any time. If you've ever gotten a "404 Error" when you try a link on a website, then you know what I'm talking about.
To solve this problem, there needs to be a standardized method of finding where something is located on the Internet, so DOI numbers were created. Again though, not all sources (especially older sources) have DOI numbers assigned to them. So what do you do?
1. If a source has an assigned DOI (whether or not it was retrieved online), the number should be included at the end of the reference.
2. If a source is retrieved online and does not have an assigned DOI, you should include the URL of the homepage of the periodical, although you do not need to include a retrieval date unless the information is updated regularly and so may change over time. This is almost never relevant for journal articles, and so I will write about this more extensively in the section covering web-based sources.
3. Finally, if a source has no assigned DOI and is not retrieved online, no DOI or URL information should (or could) be included with the reference.

Magazine article - In print or online:

You might decide to use a magazine article to provide some "pop culture" or "edgy" material to your introduction. My recommendation would be to use this source material very sparingly, and NOT in any kind of research paper. If your professor says that they want four sources used in your paper, I can guarantee you a magazine article is NOT going to count as one of them. With that warning in mind, here is how you would reference a magazine article, in this case an article about the cultural importance of the television show *Sex and the City*.

In print:
Armstrong, J. K. (2018, May 11). Sex and the City and us: How four single women changed the way we think, live, and love. *Entertainment Weekly, 1514*, 32-35.

Online:
Armstrong, J. K. (2018, May 5). Sex and the City and us: How four single women changed the way we think, live, and love. *Entertainment Weekly*. Retrieved from http://www.ew.com

You may notice that the dates are different on the "in print" and "online" editions of the same article. Both are actually correct, and my guess is that for Entertainment Weekly, information appears on their website before it appears in print. Or who knows? Print media is dead anyway.

Additionally, if you just wanted to cite the book itself rather than a magazine article about it, the book reference would look like this:

Armstrong, J. K. (2018). *Sex and the City and us: How four single women changed the way we think, live, and love.* New York, NY: Simon & Schuster.

Newspaper article - in print or online:

Newspapers, like magazines, are considered to be periodicals because they come out "periodically," usually every day. Also like magazines, newspapers can be a more up-to-date source for a particular topic, although in the following example about agoraphobia, I would question why a student is citing and referencing a newspaper article rather than reading the original article published in *Biological Psychiatry*. So, although I feel some trepidation in encouraging the use of newspapers as sources in academic papers, here is how a reference looks for a newspaper article:

In print:
Lukits, A. (2016, September 19). Fear of open spaces may be linked to animal instincts. *The Wall Street Journal*, p. D4.

Note: Page numbers for articles from newspapers should be preceded by "p." or "pp." in the reference, but this is not required for articles from magazines.

Online:
Lukits, A. (2016, September 19). Fear of open spaces may be linked to animal instincts. *The Wall Street Journal*. Retrieved from http://www.wsj.com

Books

You will find that books are a useful source when writing your paper. Books are referenced differently from periodicals and "books" are lumped together to include book chapters, encyclopedias, dictionaries, out-of-print books, and subject-specific reference books like the DSM-5. As I wrote earlier, you should NOT use encyclopedias or dictionaries as sources in your research paper; however, I feel compelled to explain how they are referenced because there are possible situations (like your professor wanting you to use dictionaries for definitions) where you will need to apply this knowledge.

Again, a generic example is pretty meaningless because every book has a different combination of authors, titles, etc., but it would look something like this:

First author last name, First author first name initial. First author middle name initial.
(#### year the book was published). *Title of the book*. Location of the publisher with city and state: Name of the publisher.

Or more simply, in an actual example of a book, as follows from the generic example:

Plunkett, J. M. (2011). *Bipolar disorder: Causes, diagnosis and treatment*. New York, NY: Nova Science Publishers.

The way authors are listed is the same for books as it is for journal articles - if a book has seven or fewer authors, list all of them in the reference; when there are eight or more authors, only the first six authors should be listed on the reference page, followed by three ellipsis points (. . .), and then the name of the last author. I haven't actually seen a book with more than seven authors, but I'm sure such a thing is possible. So here are examples of when there are various numbers of authors:

Book with one author:

Zohar, J. (2012). *Obsessive compulsive disorder: Current science and clinical practice*. Hoboken, NJ: Wiley-Blackwell. doi:10.1002/9781119941125

Note: This book is somewhat unique in that it also contains a DOI number, which are less common in books than journal articles. Where would you find the DOI number for a book? Usually on the page which lists bibliographic information, like the author, ISBN number, etc. One other thing to point out is that the DOI number is completely different from the ISBN number. The ISBN (International Standard Book Number) is a 13-digit code used in the book trade to identify the specific edition of a title, so it is different for a hardcover versus a paperback. Again, the DOI (digital object identifier) number identifies precisely where information is located within a digital network. Since most books are not online, they lack a DOI number. So, just to conclude this dissertation, while a physical book requires an ISBN, it may, or more likely, may not have an assigned DOI number. Electronic books (like Kindle books) require neither, but I'll discuss that below).

Book with two authors:

Monson, C. M., & Shnaider, P. (2014). *Treating PTSD with cognitive-behavioral therapies: Interventions that work.* Washington, DC: American Psychological Association. doi:10.1037/14372-003

Book with three authors:

Nalbantian, S., Matthews, P., & McClelland, J. (2011). *The memory process: Neuroscientific and humanistic perspectives.* Cambridge, MA: MIT Press.

Book with four authors:

Toglia, M. P., Read, J. D., Ross, D. F., & Lindsay, R. L. (2007). *The handbook of eyewitness psychology, Vol I: Memory for events.* Mahwah, NJ: Lawrence Erlbaum Associates Publishers.

Book chapters

Several things should be noted about chapters in an edited book, because this type of reference is treated as something of a hybrid of a periodical and a book. The authors' names come first (with last name and then initials, as always), then the title of the chapter, then the names of the editors ("In" with initials and THEN last name, switching things up) followed by either (Ed.) or (Eds.) depending on the number of editors. The title of the book comes next (in italics), and then the page numbers of the chapter in parentheses. The location and name of the publisher (separated by a colon) complete the reference.

Again, the way authors are listed is the same for book chapters as it was for books and journal articles - if a book has seven or fewer authors, list all of them in the reference. Examples follow:

Book chapter with one author:

Harris, D. V. (1987). Comparative effectiveness of running therapy and psychotherapy. In W. P. Morgan & S. E. Goldston (Eds.), *Exercise and mental health* (pp. 123-130). Washington, DC: Hemisphere Publishing.

Book chapter with two authors:

Coultas, J. C., & van Leeuwen, E. C. (2015). Conformity: Definitions, types, and evolutionary grounding. In V. Zeigler-Hill, L. M. Welling, T. K. Shackelford, V. Zeigler-Hill, L. M.Welling, & T. K. Shackelford (Eds.), *Evolutionary perspectives on social psychology* (pp.189-202). Cham, Switzerland: Springer International Publishing. doi:10.1007/978-3-319-12697-5_15

Ahmari, S. E., & Simpson, H. B. (2013). Neurobiology and treatment of OCD. In D. S. Charney, J. D. Buxbaum, P. Sklar, E. J. Nestler, D. S. Charney, J. D. Buxbaum, ... E. J. Nestler (Eds.), *Neurobiology of mental illness* (4th ed.) (pp. 646-661). New York, NY: Oxford University Press. doi:10.1093/med/9780199934959.003.0048

Note: I gave two examples here to illustrate a point. Although both book chapters have two authors, there are six editors for the first book on conformity and eight or more for the book on OCD. So, just as we would do for authors or books or journal articles, when there are eight or more editors of a book, only the first six editors should be listed on the reference page, followed by three ellipsis points (. . .), and then the name of the last editor. APA style is not always clear, but at least it is consistent.

Book chapter with three authors:

Mayor, J., Sainz, J., & Gonzalez-Marques, J. (1988). Stroop and priming effects in naming and categorizing tasks using words and pictures. In M. Denis, J. Engelkamp, J. E. Richardson, M. Denis, J. Engelkamp, J. E. Richardson (Eds.), *Cognitive and neuropsychological approaches to mental imagery* (pp. 69-78). Dordrecht, Netherlands: Martinus Nijhoff Publishing.

Book chapter with four authors:

Zember, E., Brainerd, C. J., Reyna, V. F., & Kopko, K. A. (2012). The science of law and memory. In E. Wethington & R. E. Dunifon (Eds.), *Research for the public good: Applying the methods of translational research to improve human health and well-being* (pp. 147-167). Washington, DC: American Psychological Association. doi:10.1037/13744-007

Wikipedia, encyclopedia, or reference work - in print or online:

This is something of a "catch-all" category in that it includes sources as diverse as Wikipedia, encyclopedias (both in print and online), dictionaries (both in print and online), subject-specific reference books, and a host of things like conference presentations (both papers and posters), dissertations, and master's theses.

Wikipedia

While I'm not going to advocate the use of Wikipedia as a reference source, as I said in the section about finding sources, Wikipedia can be a good starting place, and should probably be a part of your search strategy for an initial topic anyway. If you choose to cite Wikipedia in your paper, no date is included in the reference (n.d.) because Wikipedia is always updating, so the information may change over time. However, since Wikipedia "changes" and is updated regularly, a retrieval date is included in the reference.

As you can see from the "periodicals" section above, this is different from an online newspaper or magazine article, which will not change over time, and so needs no retrieval date information in the reference. Below is an example of how to include Wikipedia as a reference. To make things more meta, the reference is to the page covering APA style.

APA style. (n.d.). In *Wikipedia*. Retrieved June 12, 2018, from http://en.wikipedia.org/wiki/APA_style

Encyclopedia - in print:

Possibly the only thing worse than using Wikipedia as a source would be using an encyclopedia! This may come as a shock, but encyclopedias do not contain "cutting edge" information and even *Encyclopedia Britannica*, the "gold standard" of encyclopedias, stopped making a print edition in 2010 (so the 15th edition is the last one). So, using a print encyclopedia ensures that all the information is at least a decade out of date. However, if you are looking to illustrate how a topic such as "memory" has changed over time, then here is an example of how you would reference it (from my personal *World Book Encyclopedia* edition from 1920):

Memory. (1920). In *The World Book Encyclopedia*. (Vol. 6, pp. 3728-3730). Chicago, IL: W. F. Quarrie & Company.

Encyclopedia - online:

You can still find the *Encyclopedia Britannica*, but now it comes out as the *Encyclopedia Britannica Online*. My warning on using encyclopedias as sources remains in force though, as the last time an encyclopedia can be used as a source is in middle school. To keep things congruent, here is the contemporary section on the topic of memory:

Underwood, B. J. (2016). Memory. In *Encyclopedia Britannica Online*. Retrieved from
    http://www.britannica.com/topic/memory-psychology

Note: As mentioned with Wikipedia, when a URL is included in an online reference, you do not need to include a retrieval date unless the information may change over time. *Encyclopedia Britannica Online* is not constantly updated and revised, and so is dated from the last revision.

Dictionary - in print or online:

For general spelling, APA style uses the *Merriam-Webster's Collegiate Dictionary*; therefore, so should you, but only if it is absolutely necessary! A number of very poor student papers include the phrase "*Webster's* defines ____ as _____." as if they were giving a speech and believe a dictionary is an appropriate source for a college paper. It is very likely that at least one of the journal article or book sources you use for your paper will include an "operational definition" of the topic they are researching, making a dictionary a redundant source.

Dictionaries are interesting because they change between editions, with new words constantly being added. For example, in 2018, *Webster's* added 850 new words, including words such as *glamping* (a type of expensive, glamorous camping), *dumpster fire* (meaning "disaster") and *demonym* (which identifies a person as native to a place, like "Ohioan" or "Buckeye" if, like me, you're from Ohio). But where the print edition is unchanging, and has a specific edition number, the online version is constantly being revised and updated. So, here is how you would reference a dictionary:

In print:
Merriam-Webster's collegiate dictionary (11th ed.). (2005). Springfield, MA: Merriam-
    Webster.

Online:
Memory. (n.d.) In *Merriam-Webster's online dictionary*. Retrieved June 12, 2018, from
    http://merriam-webster.com/dictionary/memory

Subject-specific reference book:

Rather than using a dictionary or encyclopedia to define a term in clinical psychology, why not turn to the DSM-5? That's the latest edition of the *Diagnostic and Statistical Manual of Mental Disorders*, which is published by the American Psychiatric Association. It's not light reading, there are many pages of symptoms and mental disorders, and in reading it you are likely to begin diagnosing yourself, your friends, your family, and especially your roommates with any number of disorders that they don't have. But, if you're looking for a definition of PTSD or OCD or SAD or just about anything else in clinical psychology, here is your source:

American Psychiatric Association. (2013). *Diagnostic and statistical manual of mental disorders* (5th ed.). Arlington, VA: American Psychiatric Association.

Meetings, symposium, paper and poster presentations:

Although you are unlikely to use these as sources in your paper, you may attend a research presentation and then want to cite something you heard there. Further, when applying to graduate school, you may have presented papers (which means you gave a talk) or a poster (which means you stood by a poster and answered questions) at an undergraduate research conference, and you would want to include that in your resume.

Meetings and symposia proceedings may be published like a book or a periodical and should be referenced according to who participates, who is the Chair, and where the meeting or symposium was conducted. Unpublished paper and poster presentations (which means just about all of them) should also include information about the year, month, and location.

Symposium:

Shoda, T. M., & McConnell, A. R. (2015, May). Family as a source of support: Breadth of family inclusion and reliance in the face of stress. In S. Gabriel (Chair), *Flexible perceptions of social groups: Judgment, belongingness, and well-being consequences*. Symposium conducted at the Midwestern Psychological Association Convention, Chicago, IL.

Paper or poster presentation:

Hatala, M. N., Horton, S., Prabhu, P., Koenig, E., Kent, M., Warner, K., . . . & Rudy, M. (2014, May). *Only children: Funniest of the funny*. A poster presented at the Midwestern Psychological Association Convention, Chicago, IL.

Note: This is an actual research project that I conducted and presented with my undergraduate research assistants. There were more than eight of us on the poster, so only the first six authors should be listed in the reference, followed by three ellipsis points (. . .), and then the name of the last author. The poster was interesting because we collected demographic information on famous comedians to see if there was a pattern in their birth order - and there was! Only children (like Richard Pryor and Jerry Seinfeld) were disproportionately represented among the "top" comedians.

Doctoral dissertations, master's theses, and technical reports:

These are, again, sources that you are unlikely to use in your paper, but you may run across them while conducting a search of online psychology databases. Doctoral dissertations and master's theses are identified as such (in parentheses) after the title of the work (which is italicized). Unpublished doctoral dissertations are usually "unpublished" for a reason, and so you probably won't use them as a source.

Technical and research reports may or may not be subject to peer review and so are known as "gray" literature. They are formatted in the reference section as if they were books. The probability of you actually using one as a reference in a paper is microscopically small.

Doctoral dissertations:

Hatala, M. N. (1993). *A test of the additive unique-features model using consumer product preferences* (Unpublished doctoral dissertation). Ohio University, Athens, OH.

Note: This is my actual dissertation and it has a $20 bill taped to the title page. The last time I visited it in Ohio University's Alden Library (in 2004), the $20 bill was still there.

Dissertation abstract:

Hatala, M. N. (1993). A test of the additive unique-features model using consumer product preferences. *Dissertation Abstracts International, 54*(6-B), 3370.

Note: This is my dissertation again, but in a form that is actually accessible through online psychology databases.

Technical and research reports:

Hatala, M. N. (2015). *My year with the Narrative Clip* (Report No. 14). Greentop, MO: Greentop Academic Press.

Note: This is a fictional source as no one actually uses research reports as sources.

Audiovisual media

We're getting deeper and deeper into the weeds here, but it is theoretically possible that you would cite and then reference a documentary or television show that you had seen, and this is a very broad category of sources because audiovisual media includes not only films, television shows, and podcasts, but also artwork, maps, and photographs. Since I could fill 150 pages of examples of how the differences between citing an episode of a show versus an entire series, and something you watch on Netflix versus Amazon, I'm going to just stick to a few examples and write a different book that covers every other possible contingency.

Television show - individual episode:

Hurwitz, M., Rosenstock, R., & Martin, C. (Writers), & Chandrasekhar, J. (Director). (2004). Beef consomme [Television series episode]. In M. Hurwitz (Executive producer), *Arrested Development*. New York, NY: Fox Broadcasting.

Note: I'm a huge fan of *Arrested Development*, and this is one of the best episodes, where the characters try to find a guy named "Hermano" because they don't realize that it is Spanish for "brother."

Reviews and peer commentary:

Hatala, M. N. (2006). The therapeutic efficacy of Tobias Funke. [Review of the DVD *A guide to being an analyst and therapist*, produced by The Bluth Company, 2005]. Critical Points, 22, 203-255.

Note: This is a made-up reference related to my love of *Arrested Development*. The thing to keep in mind is that for reviews and peer commentary, the medium of what is being reviewed (such as a book or a television show) should be enclosed in brackets. If a book is being reviewed, be sure to include the author name(s) in the reference; for films or DVDs, the year that the film or DVD was released should be included in the reference.

Podcast:

Carlson, B., & Batnick, M. (2018, June 13). The Oracle of Brooklyn. [Episode 33]. *Animal Spirits* [Audio podcast]. Retrieved from http://www.awealthofcommonsense.com

Note: This is a podcast about personal finance that I like quite a bit.

Blog post:

Taylor Swift. (2014, January 15). Re: My thoughts on Greece abandoning the Euro and the response of the ECB [Web log post]. Retrieved from http://taylorswift.com/blog/abandon_the_euro.php

Note: This is obviously a "made-up" blog post (although Taylor Swift might have strong feelings about the possibility of Greece abandoning the Euro as a currency), but why are you referencing a blog post in your paper anyway?

Comment on a blog post:

Downtoclown19. (2014, January 15). Re: My thoughts on Greece abandoning the Euro and the response of the ECB [Web log comment]. Retrieved from http://taylorswift.com/blog/abandon_the_euro.php

Note: When citing material from an online community (such as a blog), if the author's name is not available, the source can be referenced by the author's screen name, in this case, Downtoclown19. If you are unfamiliar with slang, to be "down to clown" means that you are ready to enthusiastically participate in whatever activity is being proposed.

Video blog post:

PewDiePie. (2018, June 12). Someone stop this madman! [Video file]. Retrieved from http://www.youtube.com/watch?v=Q3L0gArmaE

Note: This is about the Flex Seal meme.

Music recording and music videos:

Vampire Weekend. (2013). Step. On *Modern Vampires of the City* [Vinyl record]. London, UK: XL Recordings.

This would be the citation for the vinyl record version of the song. If you prefer the compact disc version then [CD] would be appropriate, or if the song was purchased on iTunes, then [MP3 file] would be appropriate. I don't think that music groups release their albums on cassettes anymore (which means that they probably do), but if that was the version you were citing, then [Audio cassette] would be appropriate. If you want to know what Ezra Koenig is going to look like in 30 years, flip to the back cover and take a look at my picture. If you wanted to cite the music video of the song, it would be referenced as follows:

VampireWeekendVEVO. (2013, March 18). Vampire Weekend - Step [Video file]. Retrieved from http://www.youtube.com/watch?v=_mDxcDjg9P4

Social Media

Social media can be used as a source, but it can be difficult to reference because something like a Facebook post can only be accessed by someone who is a "friend" of the person who posted. That makes it classifiable as a "personal communication." So let's talk about those!

Personal communications

Personal communications include personal interviews, e-mails, telephone conversations, and private letters. Although they are infrequently a part of an academic paper, they do come up - I have personally cited emails from major figures in the field in my sabbatical applications. The person you've had the communication with should be listed by their first and middle initial and their full last name, along with the day, month, and year that the communication took place. Personal communications do not need to be included in the reference list. An example of a citation of an email I received from researcher Gordon Bell would be:

The Quantified Self (QS) movement is very much in its infancy, although a number of startup companies have entered the field (G. Bell, personal communication, August 25, 2015).

Note: Again, because this is a personal communication, it does not need to be included in your reference list.

Twitter

Famous people have been known to tweet important information, but in order to avoid any political issues, here is a tweet from Barack Obama wishing everyone a happy Mother's Day:

Obama, B. (2018, May 13). Happy Mother's Day to every mom out there, especially the remarkable moms in my life, @MichelleObama and my mother-in-law, Marian Robinson. Retrieved from http://www.twitter.com/BarackObama

Note: If you wanted to make an in-text citation of this tweet, it would look like: (Obama, 2018)

Facebook post

In keeping with non-political examples from famous people, here is a Facebook post from Barack Obama about the 2018 Obama Fellows. His account is public, so anyone can see his posts, but if he were just a "friend" of mine, then the post would be considered a "personal communication" and would not need a reference, just a citation (see above). Here is how the post would be referenced (note that it gets cut off so you don't need to write the entire post):

Obama, B. [Barack]. (2018, April 16). Each of these 20 young people have impressed me in their own unique way. Through their work around the world - from India to [Facebook status update]. Retrieved from http://www.facebook.com/pg/BarackObama/posts

Note: The author of the status update has their first name placed in brackets after their first name initial in the reference. Why? Good question! Really, it's a mystery.

Section 5 - Odds and Ends

Comparing A-F student papers

In my experience, students tend to see multiple choice exams as being "objective" because there is a correct answer. They might think that the question is "tricky" and misleading or that there are several possible answers (with one being the "best" answer), but in general, they can understand why they missed a question and why the correct answer was the "best" answer.

The grading of papers, however, is seen by students as completely "subjective" with professors handing out grades based on how much they like a student, or how long the paper is, or how tired the professor was when they were doing the grading. As someone who has read thousands and thousands of student papers over the past 25 years, I completely understand, and sometimes there is some truth to this. A professor of mine used to only read two or three papers at one sitting because after a while, "everything reads like a B-." And I realize that I have a number of "triggers" that make me irrational when I'm reading student papers: "I" statements, contractions, block quotes, using textbooks or encyclopedias as sources, and the list could go on and on. But after you've read thousands of papers, certain "objective" grading criteria begin to emerge so that you can differentiate an "A" paper from a "C" paper.

This section is intended to provide you with a professor's perspective on grading student papers. As the papers descend, they tend to have many of the same "bad" features as the other papers in their grade range and above. But it's always important to keep in mind, as I've written earlier, that there are no "bad" papers, just papers that need revision and a rewrite.

The grades are classified by the phrases ("almost perfection," "there's some good stuff here") that I have found myself writing on student papers repeatedly over the years.

The "A" paper - "Almost perfection"

This may be obvious, but "A" papers are the easiest to grade. Since they need little correction, I often find myself writing comments like "Interesting!" and "Good point!" on them so that the student knows that I'm actually reading their paper.

I know how much work it takes to get all of the little things right, so I'm grateful to my students who put the effort into handing in an "A" paper. However, there is no such thing as a "perfect paper" and even the "mandatory A+ paper" that I put at the end of this book needed some revision (and it's still not perfect).

So what are the mistakes that people who write "A" papers make? Small things, like taking a direct quote, but then not ascribing a page number to the otherwise correctly cited reference. Or a reference is missing a DOI number. These are "sins of omission" and are easily fixed. Another common error is writing out numbers that should be expressed as a numeral. For example, something like writing "seventy-two subjects" rather than "72 subjects."

As you can see, these are VERY minor problems, but problems nonetheless.

What sets an "A" paper apart from other papers is the author's comfort with the subject matter. They are able to identify the issues in a particular research topic and convey those issues to the reader. They are also familiar enough with the topic to provide informed criticism of the research, as well as provide plausible avenues of future research. They just "get it!"

So there is a sophistication and command of the material present in "A" papers that makes them stand out from the crowd.

The "B" paper - "A solid effort"

Sometimes the "B" paper is missing something. It doesn't talk about possible future research in the conclusion, or it consistently leaves the page numbers off direct quotes. At other times the "B" paper adds things that don't need to be in the paper. So they capitalize every word in the title of articles in their Reference section (which is called using the "title case"). Or when discussing authors, they include the first and middle initials rather than just addressing authors by their last names.

But the easiest way to identify "B" papers is through the use of hackneyed phrases such as "in today's society" (which always gets an eye-roll) or "it's human nature to..." (as if there was any scientific agreement on the "nature" of "human nature"). Student writers don't use these phrases because they're unintelligent; they use them because they were acceptable in high school papers, and they haven't yet "stepped up their game" to the college level. So instead of saying "in today's society," provide a statistic that highlights the point you're trying to make. Or put what you are describing as "human nature" into the context of the topic you are writing about. Sadly, "human nature" explains nothing.

For many mechanical reasons, the "B" paper is just a light edit away from being an "A" paper. However, the sophistication of the writing (such as integrating multiple studies within the same paragraph) and the level of expertise with the topic just isn't there.

The "C" paper - "There's some good stuff here!"

I'm always trying to find good things to say when I'm grading because my job isn't just to tear people's papers apart, but to find the good in them too! And there IS a lot of good in a "C" paper. The student has usually found research which is relevant to the topic, but then it's the presentation which goes wrong.

For example, "C" papers are almost always laughably conversational. They include the standard contractions (including "ain't," "didn't," and "don't"), but go a step further by actually misspelling words. Spelling errors always seem extraordinary to me because the word processing program TELLS you that you mispelled (!) the word. That means that the student knew they made a mistake, and chose to ignore it. In a college-level paper! Amazing. Perhaps they believe that their professors are not actually reading the papers?

The conversational tone isn't just about the mechanics of the writing. One of my favorite opening lines from a "C" paper about memory was "Think about the first time you ever tied your shoes - that's memory!" It's the specificity of the activity they chose which makes the example so wonderful. Of all the possible manifestations of procedural memory, they chose to focus on tying your shoes. Of course, this excludes people who wear sandals or slip-on shoes. Apparently they don't use their memory.

People who write "C" papers also like to emphasize "I" statements. While "I" statements are important in a marital counseling session (e.g. "I don't like it when you leave the cap off of the toothpaste"), they are inappropriate in a college paper. An example from a student paper might make this clearer - "I almost fully agree with Moscovici up until he says that people conform strictly to gain approval." When discussing movies, politics, or popular culture, it's great to have an opinion, but in an academic paper your professor doesn't need to know which researchers you agree with - your paper is not an analysis of a persuasive essay. There are ways to critique research without resorting to "I" statements.

Citation and reference issues are also a prominent part of "C" papers. In the body of the paper, students will often refer to researchers by their full names, and include both the institution where the research was conducted and the journal where the research was published. This is information that can be found in the References section! And speaking of the References, in a "C" paper they are often plagued by small mistakes (lack of italics, over-capitalization) that are easily corrected.

So in sum, a "C" paper has some "good stuff," but reads as if it was written as a part of an enthusiastic conversation with a friend. It has a feeling of "Hey! Have you heard about John Bowlby's research?!" rather than "Bowlby (1969) investigated the impact of strangers . . ." It's an issue of presentation. The student knows what is important, but has a difficult time communicating that information in an "academic" way.

The "D" paper - "A good rough draft"

With the "D" paper we enter the realm of students who either don't really know what they're doing, or more likely, don't care. The "D" paper isn't quite bad enough to be an "F" paper, but not for lack of trying.

What differentiates a "D" paper from an "F" paper is that the student has made an effort. Perhaps a hasty, incomplete effort, but an effort nonetheless. They have collected a set of studies, some from research journals, some from textbooks, and some from the web, but most of the sources are inappropriate for a college paper. Then they try to fit them together into a cohesive paper.

One characteristic of a "D" paper is a lack of understanding about how citation is done, so that students will often write an entire paragraph and then just put a citation at the end of it. And more often than not, the citation, although in parentheses, will have the full name of the first author and nothing else. I believe that this is because the student has seen how an academic paper is supposed to look (in my classes I provide samples of "A" papers from previous semesters), but they just don't understand what a citation is, and when it needs to be used. So the student's superficial understanding of citation (put a name in parentheses at the end of a paragraph) becomes a paper that is inappropriately written.

Another common error in "D" papers is not putting their references in alphabetical order. Again, the student knows that the last page is a list of the articles that they used in the paper, but it's unclear to them how to order the list. So some students just put them in the order that they were used in the paper. I've seen other students not alphabetize the references, but rather alphabetize the authors WITHIN each reference. The logic behind this is fascinating, but eludes me.

The final major problem that distinguishes a "D" paper is the lack of a thesis statement. Without a thesis statement, the paper is just a disorganized mess of free associations. I have seen thesis statements that say "Different experiments will be discussed and explained." Again, they know at a superficial level that they will need to include a thesis statement in their paper; they just really don't understand what that means, or how to properly execute it.

The "F" paper - "Uh oh" or "See me"

It's easy to beat up on "F" papers because the lack of student effort makes it seem deserved. And truth be told, it takes the professor longer to grade an "F" paper than the student took to write it. That's annoying. But the job of teaching writing isn't restricted to just making small corrections in otherwise perfect papers; oftentimes you just have to start over.

One of the distinguishing characteristics of the "F" paper is the lack of citation. Granted, the sources they're using for their paper are Wikipedia, encyclopedias, and textbooks, but they still manage to avoid citing them. The level of conversational general statements made by students who write "F" papers are without peer. I've seen actual sentences like "claustrophobia affects a decent sized portion of the population." Huh. Who'd a thought?

Students who write "F" papers don't pay much attention to page length requirements either. They come up with interesting and creative margins, a host of different fonts, and papers which are usually far too short (1-2 pages for a literature review). To be fair, I've also had students write 20+ pages for papers that were supposed to be 4 pages long. I stop reading after the fourth page anyway.

The Reference page of "F" papers provides only a passing resemblance to the citations made in the paper - if there are citations. The references are not alphabetized, or put in order of citation, but follow their own unique and interesting classification system.

I've seen professors get angry about students who write "F" papers because they take the lack of student effort to somehow be a sign of "disrespect" to them and their profession. I never feel this way though. Some students just don't know how to write a paper, or they have other things going on in their lives which distract them from schoolwork, or they really don't care. My job is to teach, not judge.

A word about non-sexist and non-biased writing

In my experience, students want to be thoughtful and caring, and try not to be offensive to others, both in their daily lives and in their writing. The goal of APA style is always clear and concise writing, but some students believe the APA guidelines on non-sexist and non-biased writing are an attempt to force them to be "P.C." or politically correct in their thinking. The term "freshman" is a good example. Many schools (like Yale, Dartmouth, and Cornell) now favor gender-neutral terms such as "freshperson" or just "first-year student" because they are more inclusive terms. However, APA style continues to use "freshman" because it implies a specific academic designation of someone with between zero and thirty credit hours of college credit. So you could be in your fifth year of college and still be a "freshman." The term "sophomore" is perhaps even more in need of replacement with a different term because it's etymology is a combination of the Greek words *sophos* (meaning "wise") and *moros* (meaning "fool"). Thus, a sophomore is a "wise fool." But really, who isn't?

Part of writing clearly involves using specific, acceptable, and appropriate terms for the people who participate in research. For example, "people diagnosed with depression" is appropriate, where "the depressives" or "persons with mental disorders" are not. Why? Because people are individuals and should not be identified by their conditions. In this example, people may be diagnosed with depression, but it doesn't define their existence as individuals, and so they should not be described as "the depressives." Similarly, "people diagnosed with amnesia" is appropriate; "forgetful individuals" or "persons with memory disorders" are not.

Terms for sexual orientation should be specific and sensitive, and so "lesbians" and "gay men" are acceptable, but "homosexuals" is not. This is because the term "homosexual" was used as a clinical term for decades in the Diagnostic and Statistical Manual (DSM), and it wasn't until a vote at the American Psychiatric Association Conference in 1973 that it was decided that being gay should not be considered a mental disorder (and the vote was 5,854 to 3,810). At that point the term "homosexuality" was replaced with "sexual orientation disturbance," which was thought to be more sensitive and specific because it only applied to people who were "conflicted" about their sexual orientation. I realize that this is shocking for people born in the 21st century, but it wasn't until the revision of the third edition of the DSM in 1987 that "sexual orientation disturbance" was removed as a diagnosis. Finally, I would note that "sexual orientation" is the proper term, rather than "sexual preference" because "sexual preference" implies that sexual orientation is a choice.

When it comes to non-sexist writing, "fireman" and "policeman" should be rewritten as "firefighter" and "police officer" because a person doesn't need to identify as a "man" in order to put out fires or protect the public. Similarly, terms like "mothering" should be replaced with "parenting." The use of the term "mothering" is often meant to be descriptive of "nurturing," but a person doesn't have to be a mother in order to care about children. "Waiter" and "waitress" are better described by the gender-neutral term "server," and instead of "Founding Fathers," go with "Founders." Eliminating sexist terms from our language is an ongoing process, and so I've included a list at the end of the book in Appendix C.

The terms for racial and ethnic groups follow the same logic of being specific and appropriate. For example, when writing about the earliest people of North America, "Native American," "American Indian," and "Native North American" are all acceptable. In my opinion, APA style provides minimal guidance on the complexity of race and ethnicity, except for stating that the terms used should be "parallel" (e.g. "Blacks and Whites" - as if those terms capture the diversity of the people within those designations). In general, be as specific as you need to be, so if you are studying people in Cuba, it is appropriate to refer to them as Cubans. If you are studying people from Cuba who are living in the United States, they are Cuban Americans (no hyphen). I know it may seem like I'm avoiding this issue, but acceptable terms for racial and ethnic groups are constantly evolving (a very good thing), and any guidance that I would provide would likely get ahead of where academic writing currently is, and/or would be out of date by next month.

When writing about people of different ages, the terms "girl" and "boy" are appropriate when referring to people under 12 years old, and "young woman" or "young man" (or "female adolescent" and "male adolescent") are appropriate for people between the ages of 13 and 17. At the other end of the age spectrum, the term "older adults" is appropriate; "senior citizens," "elders," and "the aged" are not.

Finally, when describing participants' actions, avoid using terms like "failed" or "unsuccessful" as they make dispositional attributions about the people who were kind enough to volunteer to be in a study. Just stick to describing research outcomes!

A note on plagiarism

The detection of plagiarism in student papers has gotten vastly easier over the past decade with the introduction of online tools such as TurnItIn.com and SafeAssign (which is a part of the Blackboard course management system used by thousands of universities). Both of these tools compare a paper not just to every journal article in their databases, but to every website, and every other paper ever submitted to the service. Then they assign a score to a paper based on how much of the text has appeared elsewhere, even if it is a direct quote and has been properly cited! It's very interesting from a professor's perspective because both tools highlight text that could be plagiarized, and then provide a footnote giving the source where the original text appears. For example, Reference sections usually get flagged by both programs because if anyone else has cited and referenced a particular source, it will be in the database and since we all use APA style for our references, it appears that everyone is plagiarizing everyone else.

It's also interesting that once a paper is submitted and becomes a part of either database, you could get flagged for rewriting one of your OWN papers that you had turned in for another class. So, for example, if you wrote a paper on conformity for your Intro to Psychology class and then used parts of the same paper in a social psychology class several years later, the program will flag that material as self-plagiarism. How much of your own work can you reuse? Good question! It's really depends on the professor, but if you are accused of self-plagiarism, always say that you have the right to use your own writing under the doctrine of "fair use." You may not get away with anything, but at least your professor will know that you have some knowledge of intellectual property law.

Most professors who have been in the academia business for a while don't need a program to detect plagiarism. The "voice" of the paper just changes, or students begin using words and phrases that make it clear that they're copying down someone else's words or ideas. They oftentimes don't understand that they've plagiarized if they've included a citation. For an extreme example, I once had a student in a Cognitive Psychology class just copy a page out of the textbook! Word for word! I'm not sure how they thought they were going to get away with that one. When confronted, they said that they thought what they did was okay because they put a citation at the end. Nope. I had another student whose SafeAssign report came back and showed that his entire paper, word for word, had been lifted from websites. He had simply put the paragraphs from different sources together with a few transitions. When confronted with the evidence of his plagiarism, he said that he didn't know how to cite and reference a website. The proper term for this in Latin boils down to "ignorance of the law is not an excuse."

Although those are two extreme examples, I have found that the vast majority of students don't intentionally plagiarize - they just don't know what they're doing. There are also numerous cases of famous writers and authors who inadvertently plagiarized, usually because they wrote from notes that were taken verbatim from sources. So how do you know when you've stepped over a line? Perhaps you're familiar with the "general rule" that's out there that if you use five identical words in a row without a direct quote citation, you've plagiarized. Well, maybe. It's not that difficult to paraphrase the writing of others; it just requires a little effort.

So let's take a look at an actual student paper on conformity. This was a "D" paper because it had numerous other issues (like the student misspelling the author they were plagiarizing). We can start out with the source they used, and then compare that to what the student wrote - the words that are plagiarized are in **bold**.

Source:
Natarajan, R. C. (2009). Halo effect in trust. *IUP Journal of Management Research*, 8(1), 26-59.

Example 1
What the student wrote:

A study by RC Natarjan demonstrates about how a **principal may trust an agent due to** either **the latter's ability to carry out the task** as **competence trust or to the perception that the latter will not act in a manner detrimental to the relationship or the former (goodwill trust).**

Natarajan (2009) source:

A principal may trust an agent either due to the latter's ability to carry out the task as desired (competence trust) or due to the perception that the latter will not act in a manner detrimental to the relationship of the former (goodwill trust).

First, be sure to correctly spell the names of the authors you are plagiarizing. Second, in a 50 word sentence, 38 of the words are "identical words in a row" without a direct quote citation. While I would admit that the source material is not the clearest writing, a corrected, non-plagiarizing paraphrasing of the same source would read as follows:

Correction:

A study by Natarajan (2009) demonstrates how a person might trust another person by either their ability to complete a task (called "competence trust") or their actions in building a relationship (called "goodwill trust").

The author is cited correctly (without including their first and middle name initials) and the sentence has been put through the "de-jargoning machine" to distill the essence of what the researcher is trying to say, while also including the critical terms they discuss.

Here's another example from the same paper, again with the words that are the same in **bold**:

Example 2
What the student wrote:

According to Natarjan, **competence trust is formed through the principal's awareness and conviction regarding the agent's skills, financial ability and consistency in performance.**

Natarajan (2009) source:

For example, competence trust is formed through the principal's awareness and conviction regarding the agent's skills, financial ability and consistency in performance - thus providing reliability.

If anything, this is an even more egregious example because in a 23 word sentence, 20 of the words are "identical words in a row." They student didn't even correct for the improper lack of an Oxford (or serial) comma after the word "ability!"

Correction:

According to Natarajan (2009), competence trust is created through "the principal's awareness and conviction regarding the agent's skills, financial ability and consistency in performance" (p. 50).

In this case, a direct quote is appropriate because there's no really good way to paraphrase this sentence. As always, quotations should be used sparingly (!), but too many properly cited quotes is better that outright plagiarism.

I hope this section has made it evident that while often inadvertent, plagiarism is easily avoided by taking the time and effort to paraphrase a source or by simply using a direct quotation.

Setting up your paper in Microsoft Word or google docs

Although many books on APA style include a section (often running 20-30 pages) on how to use Microsoft Word, google docs, and other word-processing programs to set up an APA style paper, I think that this is a topic where "showing" through an instructional video is much better than trying to learn from screen shots which are inserted into a book. Long sections on how to set up a paper using Microsoft Word are the equivalent to using "block quotes" in student writing - they're put in as unnecessary filler! Further, word-processing programs (especially ones that are available through the "cloud") change at a rapid rate - far more rapid than the books which describe how to use them. Thus, instructions on how to use word-processing programs quickly become outdated.

However, all is not lost! The following section covers the basics of how an APA style paper should be presented, and leaves it to you to work out the formatting details in the word-processing program of your choice. If you have no idea how to use a word-processing program, a very simple solution is to google "APA style google doc" or "APA style MS Word" and you will immediately be presented with a number of templates and "fill-in-the-blank" sample papers, many of which are very good! The templates are usually distributed by educators who care about the quality of student writing, and anyone who has to read student papers as a part of their job cares about the quality of student writing!

Section 6 - Do It Like This!

It's one thing to understand (or at least believe you understand) the rules of APA style, and quite another to apply them in an actual paper. This section includes two annotated research papers written in APA style - one is a student paper, and the other a journal submission.

An important distinction books on writing fail to make is the difference between "writing" your paper and "presenting" your paper. Other (vastly inferior) books just concentrate on "presenting" your paper - where do you put your academic affiliation on the title page? What are the margins on the reference page? But I think it's important to understand some general points about how the rules of APA style are applied in an actual paper.

The mandatory A+ sample paper

This section will use a student paper from my Experimental Psychology class as an "example paper," but the rules apply to any student paper written in APA style. The paper (like all student papers in this book) is reprinted with the student's permission, but I have changed the name on the paper to "Louisa May Alcott" because really, who doesn't like her writing? *Little Women* is timeless! And I'm from a generation that came before the Harry Potter books.

The paper is not perfect, but what in life is? I have seen other books that use "commentary bubbles" on sample papers, but then you can't read the paper! So I have made the decision to print the sample papers in the tradition of a translation - the actual page on the left, and the heavily annotated page on the right. That way you can see what the "comments" are "commenting" about!

As a final helpful suggestion, I have included the outline (remember when we discussed the importance of writing from an outline?!) for the paper.

Running Head: MINDFULNESS MEDITATION 1

Effectiveness of Mindfulness Meditation as a Treatment For Social Anxiety Disorder

Louisa M. Alcott

Truman State University

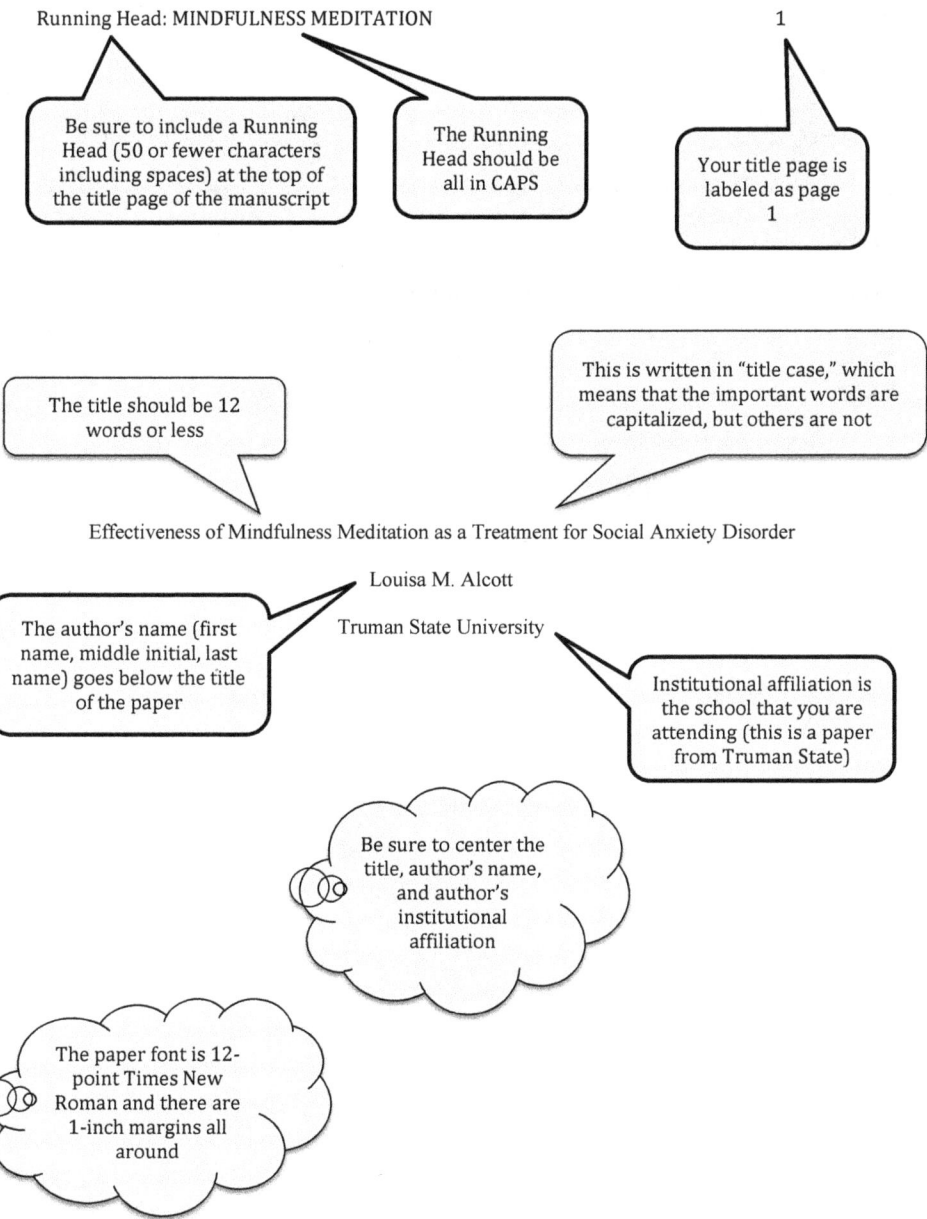

Abstract

Mindfulness meditation is an effective, low-cost treatment for social anxiety disorder (SAD). One of the main characteristics of social anxiety disorder is self-referential processing (SRP), or the tendency of those with the disorder to hyper-evaluate their own social success. SRP also results in a warped interpretation of others' body language and facial expressions, contributing to the anxiety. By emphasizing that patients focus on the moment and avoid judging any rising thoughts during the meditation, the treatment attempts to weaken the hold of SRP over SAD patients. Studies and experiments consistently demonstrate the effectiveness of mindfulness meditation as an anxiety and social anxiety treatment, including one neurological study that showed significantly less activity in SRP brain areas of social anxiety patients after a mindfulness meditation treatment. Although cognitive behavioral group therapy (CBGT) was proven a more effective treatment, mindfulness meditation is less expensive, more effective than aerobic exercise, and its effectiveness increases with practice and a spiritual focus.

Keywords: mindfulness meditation, social anxiety disorder, self-referential processing

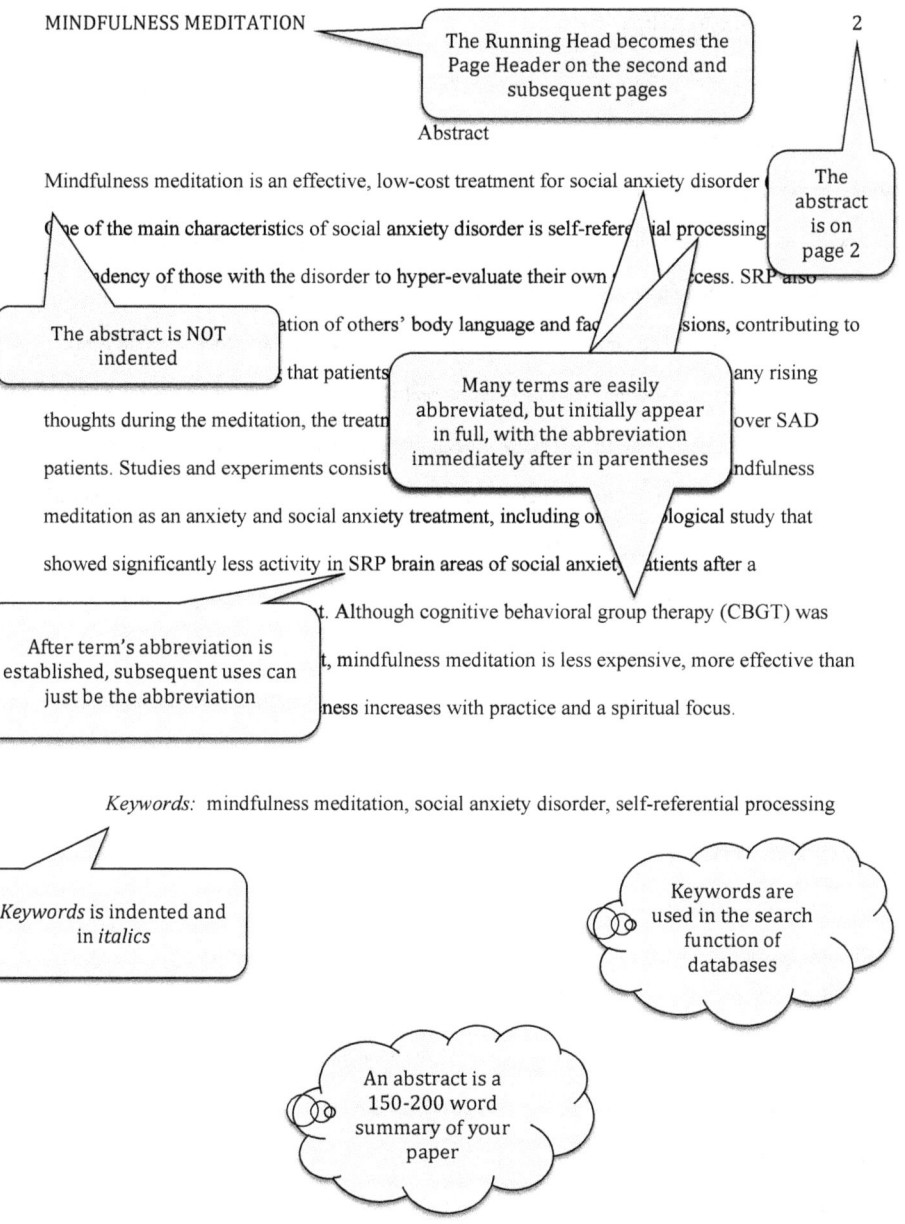

Effectiveness of Mindfulness Meditation as a Treatment for Social Anxiety Disorder

The teenage boy stumbles into a bathroom stall. He is at school, but his teary eyes, sweaty brow, and quickened breath suggest some great trauma has pushed him over the edge. His social anxiety disorder has won again. From drugs to therapy, he has tried everything to defeat his anxiety, but nothing can abate the rush of cruel faces he sees swarming his high school's halls every day. They only reflect what he expects and what he inflicts upon himself: judgment. That one word summarizes the daily internal war those afflicted with social anxiety disorder (SAD), like the teenage boy, endure. Social anxiety disorder is an intense, persistent phobia of social situations (Goldin, Ramel, & Gross, 2009), due to a heightened fixation on self-evaluation in social settings (Goldin, Ziv, Jazaieri, Hahn, & Gross, 2013). One potential treatment for social anxiety is mindfulness meditation, which involves focusing attention for a period of time without evaluating any rising thoughts (Goldin et al., 2009). In theory, the meditation could combat distorted self-judgment during social interactions, a key symptom of social anxiety. This paper evaluates the effectiveness of mindfulness meditation in treating social anxiety, compares the treatment to other treatments for social anxiety, and explores ways to improve the effectiveness of the treatment.

By learning how to acknowledge perceptions without analyzing them, mindfulness meditation can help socially anxious individuals gain control over their self-evaluation in social situations. According to Edenfield and Saeed's (2012) review of mindfulness meditation studies, gaining control over self-judgment encourages patients to socialize without as much discomfort, countering isolation and avoidance behaviors feeding the anxiety. As a treatment for social anxiety, Goldin et al. (2013) reported that mindfulness meditation has been successful, with "improved mood, functionality and quality of life in patients with SAD" (p. 244). Additionally,

Effectiveness of Mindfulness Meditation as a Treatment for Social Anxiety Disorder

    The teenage boy stumbles into a bathroom stall. He is at school, but his teary eyes, sweaty brow, and quickened breath suggest some great trauma has pushed him over the edge. His anxiety has won again. From drugs to therapy, he has tried everything to defeat what can abate the rush of emotions flooding his high school's halls every day. They only reflect what he does upon himself: judgment. That one word summarizes the daily internal war those afflicted with social anxiety disorder (SAD), like the teenage boy, endure. Social anxiety disorder is an intense, persistent phobia of social situations (Goldin, Ramel, & Gross, 2009), due to a heightened fixation on self-evaluation in social settings (Goldin, Ziv, Jazaieri, Hahn, & Gross, 2013). One potential treatment for social anxiety is mindfulness meditation, which involves focusing attention for a period and evaluating any rising thoughts (Goldin et al., 2009). In theory, the mindfulness combats distorted self-judgment during social interactions, a key symptom of social anxiety. This paper evaluates the effectiveness of mindfulness meditation on social anxiety, compares the treatment to other treatments for social anxiety, and suggests how to improve the effectiveness of the treatment.

    By learning how to acknowledge perceptions without analyzing them, mindfulness meditation helps socially anxious individuals gain control over their self-evaluation in social situations. According to Edenfield and Saeed's (2012) review of mindfulness-based therapies, gaining control over self-judgment encourages patients to socialize more as part of therapy, countering isolation and avoidance behaviors feeding the anxiety. In an empirical study on social anxiety, Goldin et al. (2013) reported that mindfulness meditation has been successful, with "improved mood, functionality and quality of life in patients with SAD" (p. 244). Additionally,

Edenfield & Saeed (2012) said in their review of mindfulness meditation research that one meta-analysis reported the treatment had a significantly greater effect than a placebo treatment.

Goldin et al. (2009) attempted to discover neurological changes in patients with social anxiety after a mindfulness meditation treatment. After recruiting 16 participants through the web and local mental health professional referrals, the patients were given a questionnaire about their mental state, then an fMRI SRP task. Since few subjects were available and the experimenters were interested in a more specific condition and treatment, they performed a small-N AB experiment, measuring patients' baseline social anxiety before mindfulness meditation and measuring it again afterwards. During the fMRI participants were flashed with a question followed by a negative or positive social trait. They pressed one of two buttons to answer whether or not a word was positive or negative, capitalized, or described themselves, depending on the question. Whether patients were evaluating themselves positively or negatively, the midline cortical brain regions and language processing areas, or regions related to self-evaluation, lit up. Goldin et al. (2009) claimed this demonstrated those with SAD "automatically rely on a ... self-focus that recruits [internal dialogue] brain systems" (p. 250) or rather, that the unhealthy self-evaluation of SAD patients is focused in those areas.

Patients then participated in eight weekly 2.5-hour sessions of mindfulness meditation, a half-day meditation retreat after session 6, and daily home practice. Experimenters monitored every subject's meditation practices daily. After the treatment, when asked to self-report their mental state again, the treatment "resulted in moderate reduction of symptoms of social anxiety, depression, rumination, and state anxiety and increased self-esteem" (Goldin et al., 2009, p. 252). At the end of 8 weeks of mindfulness meditation, patients assigned less negative social traits to themselves during the fMRI. Self-evaluation brain areas were dimmer, demonstrating the effectiveness of mindfulness meditation in reducing SRP and in extension, social anxiety.

Edenfield & Saeed (2012) said in their review of mindfulness [meditation] one meta-analysis reported the treatment had a significantly greater effect than a placebo treatment.

Goldin et al. (2009) attempted to discover neurological changes in patients with social anxiety after [mindfulness meditation], recruiting 16 participants through the web and local advertisements. Patients were given a questionnaire about their mental state, participated in an fMRI task. Since few subjects were available and the experimenters were interested in a more specific condition and treatment, they performed a small-N AB experiment, measuring patients' baseline social anxiety before mindfulness meditation and measuring it again afterwards. During the fMRI participants were flashed with a question regarding a positive or negative social trait. They pressed a button for yes or no answer for positive or negative, capitalized or lower-case. Depending on whether patients were evaluating themselves positively or negatively, the midline cortical brain regions and language processing areas, or regions related to self-evaluation, lit up. Goldin et al. (2009) claimed this demonstrated those with SAD "automatically rely on a ... self-focus that recruits [internal dialogue] brain systems" (p. 250) or rather, that the unhealthy self-evaluation of SAD patients is focused in those areas.

Patients then participated in eight weekly 2.5-hour sessions of mindfulness meditation, a half-day retreat after session 6, and daily home practice. Experimenters monitored everyone's practices daily. After the treatment, when asked to self-report their mental state again, the treatment "resulted in moderate reduction of symptoms of social anxiety, depression, rumination, and state anxiety and increased self-esteem" (Goldin et al., 2009, p. 252). At the end of 8 weeks of mindfulness meditation, patients evaluated themselves during the fMRI. Self-evaluation brain regions showed the effectiveness of mindfulness meditation in reducing

Despite mindfulness meditation's potential success as a SAD treatment, other treatments may lead to better results. In an experiment done by Koszycki, Benger, Shlik, and Bradwejn (2007), 53 SAD patients were randomly assigned to either 8 weeks of mindfulness meditation or 12 weekly sessions of CBGT. Koszyci et al. (2007) found the patients receiving CBGT had significantly lower social anxiety scores; additionally, response and remission rates were significantly greater for the CBGT group. However, in another experiment, 56 patients with generalized SAD in a randomized controlled trial were randomly assigned to 8 weeks of mindfulness meditation or 8 weeks of an aerobic exercise program (Goldin et al., 2013). An fMRI and a self-report clinical and well-being measure were given to every subject before and after the treatment (Goldin et. al, 2013). At the end of the experiment, mindfulness meditation resulted in lower self-reported social anxiety symptoms, and greater increases in the attention-regulating parietal cortical regions' neural responses, indicating greater control over negative self-judgments (Goldin et. al, 2013). Thus, mindfulness meditation proved more effective than aerobic exercise at treating SAD (Goldin et al., 2013). Although CGBT proved more effective than mindfulness meditation, mindfulness meditation could be a viable low-cost alternative to CBGT.

Additionally, there are potential ways to compensate for mindfulness meditation's lower effectiveness than cognitive therapy. According to Edenfield and Saeed's (2012) review, the more experience meditators have, the more effective meditation is at reducing anxiety. When it comes to mindfulness meditation as a treatment for SAD, practice could make perfect. One experiment found that the effectiveness of meditation depended heavily on whether or not the meditation had a religious context (Wachholtz & Pargament, 2005). Eighty-four college students were recruited for the experiment, with 25 participants in a Spiritual Meditation group, 21 participants in a Secular Meditation group, and an additional Relaxation group with 22 participants (Wachholtz &

MINDFULNESS MEDITATION 5

Despite mindfulness meditation's potential success as a SAD treatment, other treatments may lead to better results. In an experiment done by Koszycki, Benger, Shlik, and Bradwejn (2007), 53 SAD patients were randomly assigned to either 8 weeks of mindfulness meditation or 12 weekly sessions of CBGT. Koszyci et al. (2007) found the patients receiving CBGT had lower social anxiety scores; additionally, response and remission rates were higher for the CBGT group. However, in another experiment, 56 patients with generalized SAD in a randomized controlled trial received 8 weeks of mindfulness meditation or 8 weeks of an aerobic exercise program (Goldin et al., 2013). An fMRI and a self-report clinical and well-being measure were given to every subject before and after the treatment (Goldin et. al, 2013). At the end of the treatment, mindfulness meditation resulted in lower self-reported social anxiety symptoms, as well as higher attention-regulating parietal cortical regions' neural responses when reacting to negative self-judgments (Goldin et. al, 2013). Thus, mindfulness meditation was more effective than aerobic exercise at treating SAD (Goldin et al., 2013). Although CGBT proved more effective than mindfulness meditation, mindfulness meditation could be a viable low-cost alternative to CBGT.

Additionally, there are potential ways to compensate for mindfulness meditation's lower effectiveness for SAD. According to Edenfield and Saeed (2012), while meditation is an effective intervention for SAD, practice could be more perfect. One experiment found that the effectiveness of meditation depended heavily on whether or not the meditation had a religious context (Wachholtz & Pargament, 2005). Eighty-four college students were recruited for the experiment, with 25 participants in a Spiritual Meditation group, 21 participants in a Secular Meditation group, and a Relaxation group with 22 participants (Wachholtz &

Pargament, 2005). All participants practiced their technique in isolation 20 minutes a day for 2 weeks (Wachholtz & Pargament, 2005). However, the spiritual group said phrases with a religious focus as they meditated like "God is good," the secular group said positive phrases like "I am good," and the relaxation group were given no instructions for focus (Wachholtz & Pargament, 2005). Regardless of religion, those told to meditate with a religious focus showed significantly lower anxiety at the end of the experiment. Thus, a spiritual focus and meditation experience could improve mindfulness meditation results for SAD patients.

In conclusion, mindfulness meditation could provide an excellent, low-cost alternative to other SAD therapies. Although CBGT has been proven more effective as a SAD treatment, mindfulness can reduce anxiety and SRP. Additionally, through spiritual context and experience, mindfulness meditation's effectiveness can increase over time. These conclusions may not be completely valid when issues with the experiments cited are taken into account. As an AB experiment, Goldin et al.'s (2009) neurological study does not have high internal validity. Internal validity could be increased by testing the subjects after several weeks without any mindfulness meditation to see if there is a return to baseline conditions. Since it would be unethical to leave the social anxiety patients untreated, mindfulness meditation sessions would be administered again after measuring the new baseline conditions. Additionally, Wachholtz and Pargament's (2005) experiment on religious meditation vs. secular meditation did not focus specifically on social anxiety. Although a spiritual focus certainly increased the treatment's effectiveness for generalized anxiety, a religious focus might not improve meditation's impact on social anxiety. In general, more research pertaining to SAD and mindfulness meditation could be useful to truly determine the reliability of a connection between the two, as most research only explores mindfulness meditation and generalized anxiety.

Pargament, 2005). All participants practiced their technique in isolation 20 minutes a day for 2 weeks (Wachholtz & Pargament, 2005). Those told to meditate used phrases with a religious focus as they meditated, while those told to relax used positive phrases like "I am good," and the relaxation group did not meditate with any focus (Wachholtz & Pargament, 2005). Regardless of religion, those told to meditate with a religious focus showed significantly lower anxiety at the end of the experiment. Thus, a spiritual focus and meditation experience could improve mindfulness meditation results for SAD patients.

> Numerals rather than words should be used to express specific time, dates, and experimental procedures for numbers 10 and below

In conclusion, mindfulness meditation could provide an excellent, low-cost alternative to other SAD therapies. Although CBGT has been proven more effective as a SAD treatment, mindfulness can reduce anxiety and SRP. Additionally, based on personal experience, mindfulness meditation's effectiveness can improve over time. However, these results may not be completely valid when issues with the experiments cited are taken into account. As an AB experiment, Goldin et al.'s (2009) neurological study does not have high internal validity. Internal validity could be increased by testing the subjects after several weeks without any meditation to see if there is a return to baseline conditions. Since it would be unethical to leave SAD patients untreated, mindfulness meditation sessions would have to be resumed to create the new baseline conditions. Additionally, Wachholtz and Pargament's (2005) experiment on religious meditation does not focus specifically on social anxiety. Although a spiritual focus increases meditation's effectiveness for generalized anxiety, a religious focus might not improve meditation's impact on social anxiety. In general, more research pertaining to SAD and mindfulness meditation could be useful to truly determine the reliability of a connection between the two, as most research only explores mindfulness meditation and generalized anxiety.

> The conclusion is the place to insert your own perspective, as long as it is framed properly

> The conclusion is also the appropriate place to point out the shortcomings of the research reviewed

> The conclusion should also be used to discuss possible future areas of research

References

Edenfield T. M., & Saeed S., A. (2012). An update on mindfulness meditation as a self-help treatment for anxiety and depression. *Psychology Research & Behavior Management, 5*, 131-141. doi: 10.2147/PRBM.S34937

Goldin, P., Ramel, W., & Gross, J. (2009). Mindfulness meditation training and self-referential processing in social anxiety disorder: Behavioral and neural effects. *Journal of Cognitive Psychotherapy, 23*(3), 242-257. doi: 10.1891/0889-8391.23.3.242

Goldin, P., Ziv, M., Jazaieri, H., Hahn, K., & Gross, J. J. (2013). MBSR vs. aerobic exercise in social anxiety: fMRI of emotion regulation of negative self-beliefs. *Social Cognitive & Affective Neuroscience, 8*(1), 65-72. doi: 10.1093/scan/nss054

Koszycki, D., Benger, M., Shlik, J., & Bradwejn, J. (2007). Randomized trial of a meditation-based stress reduction program and cognitive behavior therapy in generalized social anxiety disorder. *Behaviour Research and Therapy, 45*(10), 2518-2526.

Wachholtz, A. B., & Pargament, K. I. (2005). Is spirituality a critical ingredient of meditation? Comparing the effects of spiritual meditation, secular meditation, and relaxation on spiritual, psychological, cardiac, and pain outcomes. *Journal of Behavioral Medicine, 28*(4), 369-384. doi: 10.1007/s10865-005-9008-5

References

Edenfield T. M., & Saeed S., A. (2012). An update on mindfulness meditation treatment for anxiety and depression. *Psychology Research & Behavior Management, 5,* 131-141. doi: 10.2147/PRBM.S34937

Goldin, P., Ramel, W., & Gross, J. (2009). Mindfulness meditation training and self-referential processing in social anxiety disorder. *Journal of Cognitive Psychotherapy, 23*(3), 242-257. doi:

Goldin, P., Ziv, M., Jazaieri, H., Hahn, K., & Gross, J. J. (2013). MBSR vs. aerobic exercise in social anxiety: fMRI of emotion regulation of negative self-beliefs. *Social Cognitive & Affective Neuroscience, 8*(1), 65-72. doi: 10.1093/scan/nss054

Koszycki, D., Benger, M., Shlik, J., & Bradwejn, J. (2007). Randomized trial of a meditation-based stress reduction program and cognitive behavior therapy in generalized social anxiety disorder. *Behaviour Research and Therapy, 45*(10), 2518-2526.

Wachholtz, A. B., & Pargament, K. I. (2005). Is spirituality a critical ingredient of meditation? Comparing the effects of spiritual meditation, secular meditation, and relaxation on spiritual, psychological, cardiac, and pain outcomes. *Journal of Behavioral Medicine, 28*(4), 369-384. doi: 10.1007/s10865-005-9008-5

Outline of mindfulness meditation paper

Introduction

    Opening – Boy stumbles into bathroom - social anxiety disorder

    Thesis statement – This paper evaluates:
        the effectiveness of mindfulness meditation in treating social anxiety,
        compares the treatment to other treatments for social anxiety,
        and explores ways to improve the effectiveness of the treatment.

Body

    Theme 1 – Effectiveness of mindfulness meditation in treating social anxiety
        Discuss Edenfield and Saeed (2012) review article
        Go in depth on Goldin, Ramel, & Gross (2009) fMRI study

    Theme 2 – Comparison with other treatments for social anxiety
        Discuss Koszycki, Benger, Shlik, & Bradwejn (2007) CGBT study

    Theme 3 – Ways to improve the effectiveness of mindfulness meditation
        Discuss Edenfield and Saeed (2012) review article on experience
        Discuss Wachholtz & Pargament (2005) study on spirituality

Conclusion
    Restatement of thesis
        Mindfulness is a low-cost alternative to other therapies

    Ideas for new research
        Discuss validity issues in Goldin, Ramel, & Gross (2009) fMRI study
        Discuss Wachholtz & Pargament (2005) and social anziety
        Propose more research on SAD and mindfulness

The mandatory "journal submission"

Although this book is titled *APA Style Basics*, I want to include a sample "journal submission" paper too, since many students have to take a psychological research course and so need to know how to present different sections of their paper (e.g. the Method, Results, and Discussion). The presentation of statistics, tables, etc., are beyond the scope of this book, but are covered in my *Learn APA Style* book, so if you're looking for more information, you might want to consult that fine publication, or if you really want to tear your hair out, consult the actual *Publication Manual of the American Psychological Association*.

The sample journal submission paper is an article that I have been unsuccessfully trying to get published for several years (well, maybe decades), so this seems like an appropriate venue for its presentation. It fills a very small niche in the literature on memory and the recall of odors, but apparently the niche is so small that journal editors have not been able to see it! This manuscript is something of a "one-off" anyway, as it does not really fit in with the rest of my research program.

To save space (and prevent extreme boredom), I have chosen not to reprint the entire manuscript, but rather the "significant" pages which begin each new section. Like the "mandatory A+ sample paper," the manuscript is far from perfect and is, after all, unpublished; however, it is a reasonable example of a journal submission, and so I've chosen to include it here. Also like the "A+ paper," I have made the decision to print the the actual page on the left, and the heavily annotated page on the right.

Running Head: ODORS AS MENTAL CUES

Odors as Mental Cues

Mark N. Hatala

Truman State University

Author Note

Mark N. Hatala, Department of Psychology, Truman State University.

The author thanks Dan Baack, Katherine Hertlein, and Tracy Mulderig for their assistance in preparing the manuscript.

Address correspondence concerning the article to Mark N. Hatala, School of Social and Cultural Sciences, Truman State University, Kirksville, Missouri 63501. E-mail: mhatala@truman.edu

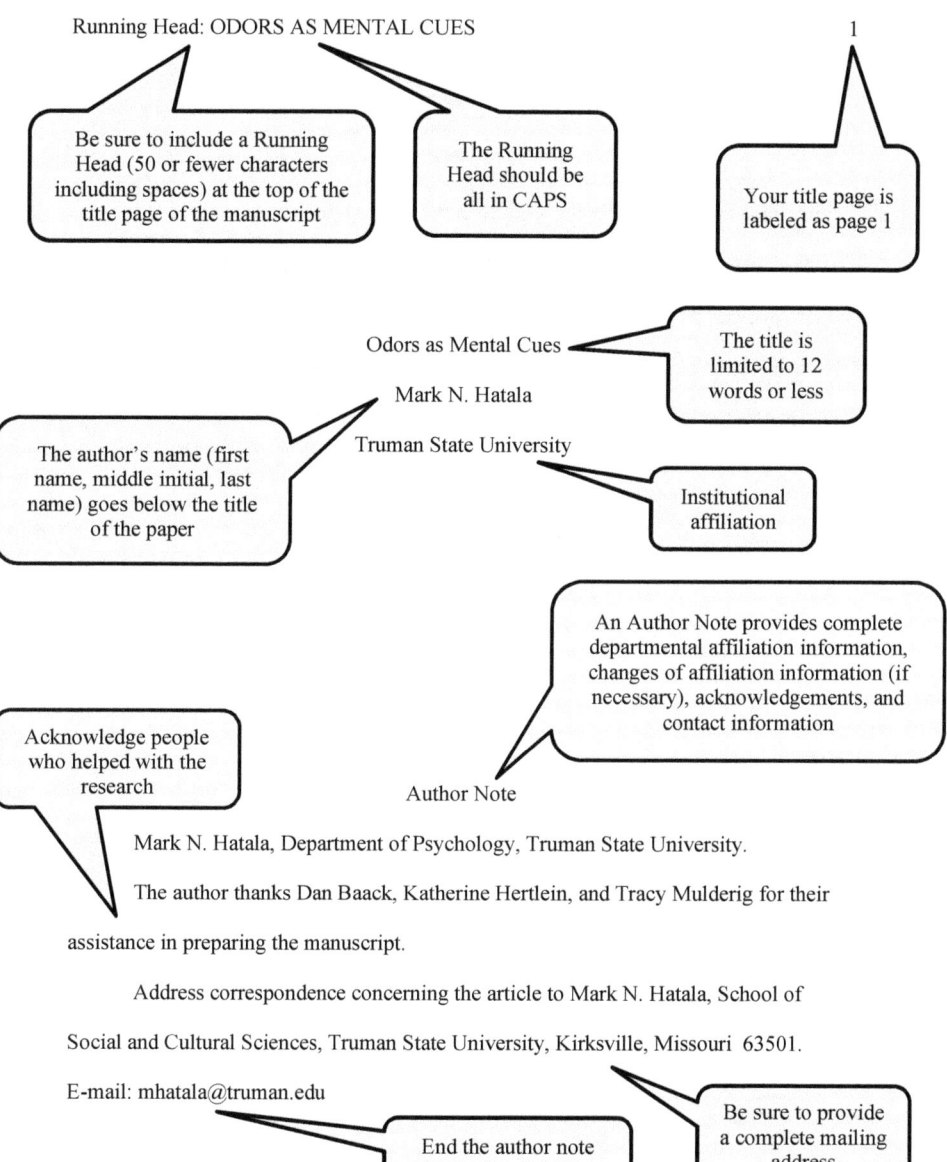

Abstract

One hundred nine subjects related concrete nouns to either names of odors or odorants and the names of the odorants. Free and cued recalls were administered after initial encoding and also one and three weeks after initial encoding. Results confirmed the hypothesis that odorants create a long-lasting memory trace. Implications for both Paivio's (1986) dual coding theory and Bellezza's (1986) mental cueing theory are discussed.

Keywords: odor, cued recall, free recall, memory, mental cueing theory

ODORS AS MENTAL CUES

Abstract

One hundred nine subjects related concrete nouns to either names of odors or odorants and names of the odorants. Free and cued recalls were administered after initial encoding and also one and three weeks after initial encoding. Results confirmed the hypothesis of a long-lasting memory trace. Implications for both Paivio's (1980) dual coding theory and Bellezza's (1986) mental cueing theory are discussed.

Keywords: odor, cued recall, free recall, memory, mental cueing theory

Odors as Mental Cues

Rudyard Kipling once said that "Smells are surer than sights or sounds to make your heartstrings crack" (cited in Smith, 1989, p. 92). The thought that odors convey emotional memories is an idea which harkens back to the ancient Greeks. Plato thought that odors could be classified in terms of their pleasantness or unpleasantness while Aristotle generally believed that if something smells good, then it is good for us; whereas if it smells bad, it is bad for us (Smith, 1989). The thought that pleasant odors bring about pleasant moods is one of the cornerstones of aroma therapy, where odors are used to bring about a positive mental state (Lawless, 1991).

Since much interest in odor has been channeled into theories of odors and emotion, relatively little research has been proposed on the interaction between odor and cognition (Herz & Eich, 1995). There may be several reasons for this. First, unlike the taste, kinesthetic, vision and auditory senses, information about odor sensation does not go directly to the thalmus, but instead is initially processed in the olfactory bulb before being passed on to the limbic system (Davis, 1977). Thus, olfactory sensations are associated more to emotional than information processing centers in the brain (Carrasco & Ridout, 1993). Second, smell is often grouped with taste and is considered to be a "lesser" sense than vision and audition (Davis, 1975). A final reason for the relative lack of cognitive research on odor deals with the fact that visual and auditory research dominates the sensation and perception literature (Annett, 1996). One author estimated that research involving odor accounted for only two percent of all studies published in sensation and perception journals (Teghtsoonian, 1983).

Although there has recently been an increase in interest as to how odor and

Odors as Mental Cues

Kipling once said that "Smells are surer than sights or sounds to make your heart-strings crack" (cited in Smith, 1989, p. 92). The thought that odors convey emotional memories is an idea which harkens back to the ancient Greeks. Plato thought that odors could be classified in terms of their pleasantness (Smith, 1989). Aristotle generally believed that if something smells good, then it is good for us, whereas if it smells bad, it is bad for us (Smith, 1989). The thought that pleasant odors bring about pleasant moods is one of the cornerstones of aroma therapy, where odors are used to alter moods and reduce stress (Buchbauer, Jirovetz, Jager, Plank, & Dietrich, 1991). Although much research has been channeled into theories of odors and emotion, relatively little research has been proposed on the interaction between odor and cognition (Herz & Eich, 1995). There may be several reasons for this. First, unlike the taste, kinesthetic, vision and auditory senses, information about odor sensation does not go directly to the thalamus, but instead is initially processed in the olfactory bulb before reaching the limbic system (Davis, 1977). Thus, olfactory sensations are more related to emotional than information processing centers in the brain (Carrasco & Ridout, 1993). Second, smell is often grouped with taste and is considered to be a "lesser" sense than vision and audition (Carrasco & Ridout, 1993). The relative lack of cognitive research on odor cognition is reflected by research. Vision research dominates the sensation and perception literature, and one author estimated that research involving odor accounted for only two percent of all studies published in sensation and perception journals (Teghtsoonian, 1983).

Although there has recently been an increase in interest as to how odor and

This research also has important implications for mental cueing theory (Bellezza, 1986). In this experiment, odors are used as part of a cognitive cueing structure to facilitate the recall of concrete nouns.

Method

Participants

One hundred eight subjects from psychology courses at Truman State University volunteered to participate for extra course credit. As this experiment required subjects to return one and three weeks after the initial learning session, five subjects who were not able to attend all testing sessions were eliminated from the experiment.

Materials

A set of olfactory stimuli was constructed using common household odors. The fifty odors used (for a list of odors, see Appendix A) were drawn from odors sets typically used by other researchers (Schab & Crowder, 1995; Lyman & McDaniel, 1986). Odorants were placed into 250-ml odorless plastic bottles which had pull-up spouts. The bottles were opaque, but were nonetheless covered with masking tape so that subjects could not identify the contents of the bottles. This is important because Zellner & Kautz (1990) have found that the color of a stimulus could be a valuable cue in odor identification.

The odor was released from the bottle by pulling up the spout and squeezing the bottle under the nose. Each of the bottles had a number on it which corresponded to a 3" by 5" index card which contained the number and name of the odorant on opposite sides.

The 50 concrete nouns used in the experiment were randomly selected from a

This research has implications for mental cueing theory (Bellezza, 1986). In this experiment, the use of a cognitive strategy was examined to facilitate the recall of olfactory stimuli.

Method

Participants

One hundred eight subjects from psychology courses at Truman State University volunteered to participate for extra course credit. As this experiment required subjects to return one and three weeks after the initial learning session, five subjects who were not able to attend all testing sessions were eliminated from the experiment.

Materials

A set of olfactory stimuli was constructed using fifty odors. The fifty odors used (for a list of odors, see Appendix A) were drawn from odors sets typically used by other researchers (Schab & Crowder, 1995; Lyman & McDaniel, 1986). Odorants were placed into 250-ml odorless plastic bottles. The bottles were opaque, but were nonetheless covered with tape so that subjects could not identify the contents of the bottles. This is important because Zellner & Kautz found that visual aspects of a stimulus could be a valuable cue in odor identification.

The odor was released from the bottle by pulling up the spout and squeezing the bottle under the nose. Each of the bottles had a number label attached and a 3" by 5" index card which contained the number and name of the odorant on opposite sides.

The 50 concrete nouns used in the experiment were randomly selected from a cued or free recall of the list words. In the cued recall, subjects were encouraged to go from table to table looking at the names of the odors, whereas in the free recall they had to just try to remember the names of the 50 odors. Subjects were then debriefed and dismissed.

Subjects were invited back for a cued or free recall (depending on which they had performed at the initial encoding session) both one week and three weeks after the initial encoding session. Again, for the cued recall, they were encouraged to go around to all of the tables and smell the odorants or look at the cards (depending on the group that they were in). Subjects in the free recall condition just sat and recalled as many of the 50 list words as they could for eight minutes.

Results

List word recall for the first experimental session was examined with a 2 x 2 (Odor [odorants and odor names, odor names] x Recall [cued, free]) analysis of variance (ANOVA). Results revealed a strong main effect for the recall condition, $F(1, 104) = 79.26, p < .0001, \eta_p^2 = .74$, but no effect for the use of odorants at encoding. In line with hypotheses about initial recall, subjects who were given a cued recall at the initial recall session were able to recall far more words than subjects who were asked to perform just a free recall. This can be seen clearly in Table 1 below. These results, however, must be interpreted in light of a significant 2-way interaction, $F(1, 104) = 5.33, p < .02, \eta_p^2 = .04$.

Results for familiarity and pleasantness ratings were mixed. When looking at familiarity ratings of all 50 odors, there were no effects for odor or recall condition; however, when examining the pleasantness ratings, subjects who received both the odor and odor name rated the odors as being less pleasant than subjects who just received the cued or free recall of the list words. In the cued recall, subjects moved from table to table looking at the names of the odors, whereas in the free recall they had to remember the names of the 50 odors. Subjects were then debriefed and

Subjects were invited back for a cued or free recall (depending on which they had in their initial encoding session) both one week and three weeks after the initial session. Again, for the cued recall, they were encouraged to go around to all of the tables, smell the odorants or look at the cards (depending on which group they were in). Subjects in the free recall condition just sat and recalled as many words as they could for eight minutes.

Results

List word recall for the first experimental session was examined with a 2 x 2 (Odor [odorants and odor names, odor names] x Recall [cued, free]) analysis of variance (ANOVA). Results revealed a strong main effect for the recall condition, $F(1, 104) = 79.26$, $p < .0001$, , $\eta_p^2 = .74$, but no effect for the use of odorants at encoding. In line with hypotheses, without initial recall, subjects who were given an odor at the encoding session recalled more words than subjects who did not, as can be seen in Table 1 below. These results, however, must be interpreted in light of a two-way interaction, $F(1, 104) = 5.33$, $p < .02$, $\eta_p^2 = .04$.

Results for familiarity and pleasantness ratings were mixed. When looking at familiarity ratings of all 50 odors, there were no effects of any of the variables; however, when examining the pleasantness ratings, subjects who received both odor and odor name rated the odors as being less pleasant than subjects who just received the odor names, $F(1, 104) = 8.06$, $p < .005$, $\eta_p^2 = .15$. This suggests that while familiarity is unaffected by memory, subjects have more pleasant memories of odors than when they are actually presented with those odors.

Analyses which examine familiarity and pleasantness ratings for words which were and were not recalled showed no differences between the groups, as can be seen in Table 2.

Discussion

Results confirmed the hypothesis that initial recall would have a strong main effect for recall condition, with cued recall outperforming free recall. There was no difference between groups as to whether they received odors at encoding or not. This seems logical and was predicted because although subjects who get both the odor name and the odor may have better elaboration, the subjects who did not receive the olfactory stimuli had more time to construct better sentences. Although there was a significant interaction, it was mostly driven by the significant main effect for recall condition. The omega squared value for the recall condition main effect is .745, while the omega squared value for the interaction is .041. Thus, at the time of initial recall, odor plays a negligible role in the recall process.

The pleasantness ratings of the odors are interesting because people who actually received the odors rated them as less pleasant than subjects who did not receive the odors. Perhaps memories for common household odors are stored as some sort of abstract, idealized prototype, so that the actual odor when presented is not as pleasant as we remember.

odor names, $F(1, 104) = 8.06$, $p < .005$, $\eta_p^2 = .15$. This suggests that while familiarity is unaffected by memory, subjects have more pleasant memories of odors than when they are actually presented with those odors.

Analyses ... pleasantness ratings for words which were and were ... between ... Table 2.

> *Provide the obtained value of the statistic, the degrees of freedom, the p-vlaue, and the effect size*

> *The Discussion heading is centered and in boldface*

Discussion

Results confirmed the hypothesis that initial recall would have a strong main effect for recall condition, with cued recall ... There was no difference between groups as to whether ... coding or not. This seems logical ... was predicted because although subjects who get both the odor name ... better elaboration, the subjects who did not receive the olfactory ... construct better sentences. Although there was a significant ... driven by the significant main effect for recall condition. The omega squared value for the recall condition main effect is .745, while the omega squared value for the interaction is .041. Thus, at the time of initial recall, odor plays a negligible role in the recall process.

> *Be sure to clearly identify tables by number*

> *The Discussion should "discuss" whether experimental hypotheses were supported*

The pleasantness ratings of the odors are interesting because people who actually received the odors rated them as less pleasant than subjects who did not receive the odors. Perhaps memories for common household odors ... ract, idealized prototype, so that the actual odor when ... we remember.

> *Interpret results in the present tense in order to bring the reader into the "discussion"*

References

Algom, D. A., & Cain, W.S. (1991). Remembered odors and mental mixtures: Tapping reservoirs of olfactory knowledge. *Journal of Experimental Psychology: Human Perception and Performance, 17,* 1104-1119.

Annett, J. M. (*1996*). Olfactory memory: A case study in cognitive psychology. *The Journal of Psychology, 130,* 309-319.

Annett, J. M., McLaughlin Cook, N., & Leslie, J. C. (1995). Interference with olfactory memory by visual and verbal tasks. *Perceptual and Motor Skills, 80,* 1307-1317.

Bellezza, F. S. (1983). Mnemonic device instruction with adults. In M. Pressley, & J. R. Levin (Eds.), *Cognitive strategy research: Psychological foundations* (pp. 51-73). New York, NY: Springer-Verlag.

Bellezza, F. S. (1986). Mental cues and verbal reports in learning. In G. H. Bower (Ed.), *The psychology of learning and motivation* (Vol. 20, pp. 237-273). New York, NY: Academic Press.

Bellezza, F. S. (1987). Mnemonic devices and memory schemas. In M. McDaniel & M. Pressley (Eds.), *Imaginal and mnemonic processes* (pp 34-55). New York, NY: Springer-Verlag.

Bellezza, F. S., & Buck, D. K. (1988). Expert knowledge and mnemonic cues. *Applied Cognitive Psychology, 2,* 147-162. doi: 10.1002/acp.2350020206

Bellezza, F. S., & Hoyt, S. K. (1992). The self-reference effect and mental cueing. *Social Cognition, 10,* 51-78. doi: 10.1521/soco.1992.10.1.51

Bolger, E. M., & Titchener, E. B. (1907). Some experiments on the associative power of smells. *American Journal of Psychology, 18,* 326-327.

References

Algom, D. A., & Cain, W.S. (1991). Remembered odors and mental reservoirs of olfactory knowledge. *Journal of Experimental Perception and Performance, 17,* 1104-1119.

Annett, J. M. (1996). Olfactory memory: A case study in cognition. *The Journal of Psychology, 130,* 309-319.

Annett, J. M., McLaughlin Cook, N., & Leslie, J. C. (1995). Interference with olfactory memory by visual and verbal tasks. *Perceptual and Motor Skills, 80,* 1307-1317.

Bellezza, F. S. (1983). Mnemonic device instruction with adults. In M. Pressley, & J. R. Levin (Eds.), *Cognitive strategy research: Psychological foundations* (pp. 51-73). New York, NY: Springer-Verlag.

Bellezza, F. S. (1986). Mental cues and verbal reports in learning. In G. H. Bower (Ed.), *The psychology of learning and motivation* (Vol. 20, pp. 237-273). New York, NY: Academic Press.

Bellezza, F. S. (1987). Mnemonic devices and memory schemas. In M. McDaniel & M. Pressley (Eds.), *Imaginal and mnemonic processes* (pp 34-55). New York, NY: Springer-Verlag.

Bellezza, F. S., & Buck, D. K. (1988). Expert knowledge and mnemonic cues. *Applied Cognitive Psychology, 2,* 147-162. doi: 10.1002/acp.2350020206

Bellezza, F. S., & Hoyt, S. K. (1992). The self-reference effect and mental cueing. *Social Cognition, 10,* 51-78. doi: 10.1521/soco.1992.10.1.51

Bolger, E. M., & Titchener, E. B. (1907). Some experiments on the associative power of smells. *American Journal of Psychology, 18,*

Appendices A-C

I decided to reproduce the following three brief sections from my *Learn APA Style* book because they work as a reference when you need a quick answer to a question like "What font does APA style use?" or "What's the non-sexist term for mailman?"

The "APA style in a nutshell" section is a distillation of the *Publication Manual of the American Psychological Association* from 272 pages down to four. Surprisingly, little is lost in the process. Parenthetical comments refer to the section and page numbers in the *Publication Manual* where that information appears. The other two sections are about abbreviations and non-biased and non-sexist terms. I also put an index at the end of the book to help find things quickly.

Best of luck to you in your writing!

APA style in a nutshell

We know what we are trying to say, but it can be difficult to know the correct way to say it. That's where APA style comes in. It is basically a set of rules designed to provide the framework for scientific publication.

For many students, APA style boils down to learning how to set up the margins of a paper and how to correctly compose the references at the end. Unfortunately, that is all the guidance that most books offer too. In this very brief section, the object is to distill APA style down to the essentials - a "cheat sheet" of literary style. When section and page numbers appear, they refer to the corresponding sections and pages of the sixth edition of the *Publication Manual of the American Psychological Association*.

Formatting

APA style requires a 12-point Times New Roman typeface that is double-spaced with 1 inch margins all around (top, bottom, left, right) the manuscript; however, in a figure the typeface should be Arial, Futura, or Helvetica (5.25 - page 161) no smaller than 8-point and no larger than 14-point.

Do NOT print on both sides of an APA style paper (even though it saves paper).

The recommended length for the title of a manuscript is 12 words or less (2.01 - page 23). The title should be centered and capitalized (at least the important words).

Word limits for abstracts vary depending on the journal, but are generally between 150 to 250 words (2.04 - page 27).

The institutional affiliation listed on the manuscript is where the author or authors were when the research was conducted (2.02 - page 23).

The preferred form of the author's name (or byline) is first name, middle name initial(s), last name (2.02 - page 23).

A complete mailing address for correspondence about the manuscript as well as any possible conflicts of interest appear in the author note (2.03 - page 25).

A simple representation of the order of components in a manuscript would be: Title page (which includes the RUNNING HEAD, title, author names, institutional affiliations, and author note), abstract, Introduction, Methods, Results, Discussion, References, and supplementary materials (such as Tables and Figures) and Appendices .

The title page is page 1, the abstract begins on page 2, and the introduction begins on page 3. The following sections (Methods, Results, and Discussion) are continuous and do not need to start on their own pages. The References should begin on a new page (with References centered, but not in bold). Supplementary materials (e.g. tables and figures) should each appear on their own page.

The Method, Results, and Discussion sections should be centered and in bold.

Authors should incorporate a direct quotation into the text if the quote contains fewer than 40 words. More than 40 words and it should be inserted as a block quotation (6.01 - page 170).

Citations and references

Books and journal articles will make up 90% of your references. Here is what they should look like:

For an article on the topic of bystander intervention:
Garcia, S. M., Weaver, K., Moskowitz, G. B., & Darley, J. M. (2002). Crowded minds: The implicit bystander effect. *Journal of Personality and Social Psychology*, *83*(4), 843853. doi:10.1037/00223514.83.4.843

For a book on the topic of bystander intervention:
Latane, B., & Darley, J. (1970). *The Unresponsive bystander: Why doesn't he help?* New York, NY: Prentice Hall.

The first line of each reference is "flush left," which means it begins at the left margin. Subsequent lines are indented five spaces (or ½ inch).

When a manuscript has three or more authors, subsequent citations (after the first citation) should always include the last name of the first author followed by et al.

If you cite two or more works within the same set of parentheses, they should be in alphabetical order (6.16 - page 177).

Every entry in an APA style reference list contains all of the following elements: author(s), year of publication, title, and publishing data (6.22 - page 180).

If a direct quotation contains a citation, you should include the citation, but not include it in your references.

All references that are cited in a text also have to appear in the reference list except for classical works (like the Bible) and personal communications.

When there are eight or more authors on a single paper, only the first six authors should be included in the references, followed by three ellipsis points, and then the name of the last author.

For example:
Fischer, P., Greitemeyer, T., Kastenmuller, A., Krueger, J. I., Vogrincic, C., Frey, D., . . . Kainbacher, M. (2011). The bystander effect: A meta-analytic review on bystander intervention in dangerous and nondangerous emergencies. *Psychological Bulletin, 137*(4). 517537. doi: 10.1037/a0023304

If a DOI is assigned to a source that you reference, you should include the DOI at the end of the reference (7.01 - page 198).

If there is no DOI assigned to a periodical, and it was retrieved online, no retrieval date is needed.

If a DOI has not been assigned to a periodical that you retrieved online, you should include the homepage URL of the periodical in your reference (7.01 - page 198).

If a book has no author or editor, it should be alphabetized by the first significant word of the title.

If you use a source and cannot find an appropriate "APA style" way to reference it, you should choose an APA example that is similar to your source and follow that format.

Writing and publishing

The names of the authors of a manuscript appear in the order of their contributions to the work (1.13 - page 19).

A work is copyrighted from the moment it is typed on a page by the author (1.15 - page 9).

After publication, by law, publishers own the copyright on their journal articles for 95 years from the date of publication (8.05 - page 236).

Taking someone else's work and presenting it as your own is the very definition of plagiarism (1.10 - page 15).

When discussing the implications of the results, be sure to use the present tense (3.06 - page 66).

Results are described using the past tense (3.06 - page 66).

"Girl" and "boy" are considered appropriate terms for referring to individuals under 12 years old (3.16 - page 76).

An effective way to achieve the right tone in a scientific manuscript is to imagine that you are writing for a researcher in a related field (3.07 - page 67).

The number of members in a total sample is represented by an uppercase, italicized N (4.45 - page 118).

In general, numerals should be used to express numbers 10 and above (4.31 - page 111). In general, words should be used to express numbers below 10 (4.31 - page 111). Numbers should be spelled out if they begin a sentence.

When possible, all physical measurements should use the metric system (4.39 - page 114).

Tables and figures are labelled separately, so you could have a Table 1 and a Figure 1.

If tables and figures are included in an appendix, they would be labelled as follows: Table A1, Table A2, Table A3 (5.05 - page 127).

Any data display that's not a table is referred to as a figure (5.01 - page 125).

An example of the proper way to refer to a table in a manuscript would be "as can be seen in Table 1." (5.10 - page 130).

The review process for an academic manuscript usually takes approximately two to three months (8.01 - page 226).

The final editorial authority of a journal (as to whether or not a manuscript is accepted for publication) lies with the editor (8.01 - page 226).

APA-approved list of abbreviations

Acquired Immune Deficiency Syndrome	AIDS
alternating current	AC
American College Testing	ACT
American Psychological Association	APA
analysis of variance	ANOVA
Attention Deficit Hyperactivity Disorder	ADHD
body mass index	BMI
centimeter	cm
conditioned response	CR
conditioned stimulus	CS
consonant-vowel-consonant	CVC
decibel (scale)	dB
degrees of freedom	df
direct current	DC
Doctor of Philosophy	Ph.D.
electronic mail	e-mail
extra-sensory perception	ESP
frequency	f
Graduate Record Exam	GRE
hertz	Hz
hour	hr
Human Immunodeficiency Virus	HIV
hypertext transfer protocol	http
intelligence quotient	IQ
kilogram	kg
kilometer	km
kilowatt	kW
liter	L
long-term memory	LTM

meter (unit of measurement)	m
miles per hour	mph
milligram	mg
milliliter	ml
millimeter	mm
millisecond	ms
Minnesota Multiphasic Personality Inventory	MMPI
minute	min
multivariate analysis of covariance	MANCOVA
Pearson product-moment correlation	r
portable document format	PDF
rapid eye movement	REM
reaction time	RT
Scholastic Aptitude Test	SAT
second (as in time unit)	s
short-term memory	STM
sum of squares	SS
total number of cases	N
uniform resource locator	URL
volt	V
watt	W

List of non-sexist and non-biased terms

Afro-American	African-American
amnesiacs	amnesic patients
anchorman	anchor
ancient man	ancient civilization
calendar girl	model
call girl	escort, prostitute, sex worker
cameraman	camera operator
cleaning lady	cleaner
coed	student
cowboy	cowhand
the common man	the average or typical person
congressman	congressional representative or member of congress
the elderly	older adults
Father of Psychology (or any other academic field)	Founder of Psychology
fireman	firefighter
foreman	supervisor
Founding Fathers	Founders
handicapped	disabled
homosexual man	gay man
homosexual woman	lesbian
housewife	homemaker
mailman	postal worker or mail carrier
male nurse	nurse
man and wife	husband and wife
man's best friend	alcohol
mankind	humanity
men of science	scientists
mothering	parenting
newspaperman	journalist
police woman	police officer
retarded	developmental disabilities
senility	dementia
sex change	sex reassignment
sexual preference	sexual orientation
stewardess	flight attendant
tax man	tax collector
transvestite	cross-dresser
policeman	police officer
waitress	server

Body image

Feingold, A., & Mazzella, R. (1998). Gender differences in body image are increasing. *Psychological Science, 9*(3), 190-195.

Grabe, S., Ward, L.M., & Hyde, J.S. (2008). The role of the media in body image concerns among women: A meta-analysis of experimental and correlational studies. *Psychological Bulletin, 134*(3), 460-476. doi:10.1037/0033-2909.134.3.460

Hamilton, E., Mintz, L., & Kashubeck-West, S. (2007). Predictors of media effects on body dissatisfaction in European American women. *Sex Roles, 56*(5/6), 397-402. doi: 10.1007/s11199-006-9178-9

Hamilton, S. R. (2008). A relationship between perceived body image and depression: How college women see themselves may affect depression. *Student Journal of Psychological Science, 1*(1), 13-20.

Hargreaves, D. A. & Tiggemann, M. (2009). Muscular ideal media images and men's body image: Social comparison processing and individual vulnerability. *Psychology of Men and Masculinity, 10*(2), 109-119. doi: 10.1037/a0014691

Harrison, K. (2003). Television viewers' ideal body proportions: The case of the curvaceously thin woman. *Sex Roles, 48*, 255–264.

Kopcakova, J., Dankulincova Veselska, Z., Madarasova Geckova, A., van Dijk, J. P., & Reijneveld, S. A. (2014). Is being a boy and feeling fat a barrier for physical activity? The association between body image, gender and physical activity among adolescents. *International Journal of Environmental Research and Public Health, 11*(11), 11167–11176. doi:10.3390/ijerph111111167

Lawrie, Z., Sullivan, E. A., Davies, P. W., & Hill, R. J. (2006). Media influence on the body image of children and adolescents. *Eating Disorders, 14*(5), 355-364. doi: 10.80/10640260600952506.

Rancour, P., & Brauer, K. (2003). Use of letter writing as a means of integrating an altered body image: A case study. *Oncology Nursing Forum, 30*(5), 841-846.

Ricciardelli, L., & Williams, R. (2014). Social media and body image concerns: Further considerations and broader perspectives. *Springer Science & Business Media B.V., 71*(11), 389-392. doi: 10.1007/s11199-014-0429-x

Rosenblum, G. D, & Lewis, M. (1999). The relations among body image, physical attractiveness, and body mass in adolescence. *Child Development, 70*(1), 50-64.

Woertman, L., & Brink, F. (2012). Body image and female sexual functioning and behavior: A review. *The Journal of Sex Research, 49*(2-3),184-211.

Bystander effect

Aboud, F. E., & Joong, A. (2008). Intergroup name-calling and conditions for creating assertive bystanders. In S. R. Levy & M. Killen (Eds.), *Intergroup attitudes and relations in childhood through adulthood* (pp. 249-260). New York, NY: Oxford University Press.

Barnett, V. (1999). *Bystanders: Conscience and complicity during the Holocaust.* Westport, CT: Greenwood Press.

Byers, D. S. (2013). 'Do they see nothing wrong with this?': Bullying, bystander complicity, and the role of homophobic bias in the Tyler Clementi case. *Families in Society, 94*(4), 251-258. doi:10.1606/1044-3894.4325

Fischer, P., Greitemeyer, T., Kastenmuller, A., Krueger, J. I., Vogrincic, C., Frey, D., . . . Kainbacher, M. (2011). The bystander-effect: A meta-analytic review on bystander intervention in dangerous and non-dangerous emergencies. *Psychological Bulletin, 137*(4). 517-537. doi: 10.1037/a0023304

Garcia, S. M., Weaver, K., Moskowitz, G. B., & Darley, J. M. (2002). Crowded minds: The implicit bystander effect. *Journal of Personality and Social Psychology, 83*(4), 843-853. doi:10.1037/0022-3514.83.4.843

Greitemeyer, T., & Mügge, D. (2013). Rational bystanders. *British Journal of Social Psychology, 52*(4), 773-780. doi:10.1111/bjso.12036

Howard, W. & Crano, W. D. (1974). Effects of sex, conversation, location, and size of observer group on bystander intervention in a high risk situation. *Sociometry, 37*(4). 491-507.

Hudson, J., & Bruckman, A. (2004). The bystander effect: A lens for understanding patterns of participation. *The Journal of the Learning Sciences, 13*(2), 165-195.

Huston, T. L., Ruggiero, M., Conner, R. & Geis, G. (1981). Bystander intervention into crime: A study based on naturally-occurring episodes. *Psychology Quarterly, 44*(1). 14-23.

Latane, B., & Darley, J. (1970). *The unresponsive bystander: Why doesn't he help?* New York, NY: Prentice Hall.

Nelson, J. K., Dunn, K. M., & Paradies, Y. (2011). Bystander anti-racism: A review of the literature. *Analyses of Social Issues and Public Policy, 11*(1), 263-284. doi:10.1111/j.1530-2415.2011.01274.x

Tice, D. M., & Baumeister, R. F. (1985). Masculinity inhibits helping in emergencies: Personality does predict the bystander effect. *Journal of Personality and Social Psychology, 49*(2), 420-428. doi:10.1037/0022-3514.49.2.420

Stürmer, S., & Snyder, M. (2009). *The psychology of prosocial behavior: Group processes, intergroup relations, and helping.* Malden, MA: Wiley-Blackwell.

Conformity

Asch, S. E. (1951). Effects of group pressure upon the modification and distortion of judgment. In H. Guetzkow (Ed.), *Groups, leadership and men: Research in human relations*. Pittsburgh, PA: Carnegie Press.

Bond, R., & Smith, P. B. (1996). Culture and conformity: A meta-analysis of studies using Asch's (1952b, 1956) line task. *Psychological Bulletin, 119*(1), 111-137.

Campbell, J. D., & Fairey, P. J. (1989). Informational and normative routes to conformity: The effect of faction size as a function of norm extremity and attention to the stimulus. *Journal of Personality and Social Psychology, 57*, 457-468.

Cialdini, R. B., & Goldstein, N. J. (2004). Social influence: Compliance and conformity. *Annual Review of Psychology, 55*, 591-621.

Cooper, H. M. (1979). Statistically combining independent studies: A meta-analysis of sex differences in conformity research. *Journal of Personality and Social Psychology, 37*(1), 131-146. doi:10.1037/0022-3514.37.1.131

Coultas, J. C., & van Leeuwen, E. C. (2015). Conformity: Definitions, types, and evolutionary grounding. In V. Zeigler-Hill, L. M. Welling, T. K. Shackelford, V. Zeigler-Hill, L. M.Welling, & T. K. Shackelford (Eds.), *Evolutionary perspectives on social psychology* (pp.189-202). Cham, Switzerland: Springer International Publishing. doi:10.1007/978-3-319-12697-5_15

Eagly, A. H. (1987). *Sex differences in social behavior: A social role interpretation*. Hillsdale, NJ: Erlbaum.

Eagly, A. H., & Carli, L. L. (1981). Sex of researchers and sex-typed communications as determinants of sex differences in influenceability: A meta-analysis of social influence studies. *Psychological Bulletin, 90*(1), 1–20.

Gerald, H. B., Wilhemy, R. A., & Conolley, E. S. (1968). Conformity and group size. *Journal of Personality and Social Psychology, 8*(1), 79-82.

Maslach, C., Santee, R. T., & Wade, C. (1987). Individuation, gender role, and dissent: Personality mediators of situational forces. *Journal of Personality and Social Psychology, 53*(6), 1088-1093. doi:10.1037/0022-3514.53.6.1088

Neto, F. (1995). Conformity and independence revisited. *Social Behavior and Personality: An International Journal, 23*(3), 217-222.

Pasupathi, M. (1999). Age differences in response to conformity pressure for emotional and nonemotional material. *Psychology and Aging, 14*(1), 170-174. doi:10.1037/08827974.14.1.170

Santee, R. T. & Jackson, S. E. (1982). Identity implications of conformity: Sex differences in normative and attributional judgments. *Social Psychology Quarterly, 45*(2), 121-125.

Stowell, J.R., Oldham, T., & Bennett, D. (2010). Using student response systems ("clickers") to combat conformity and shyness. *Teaching of Psychology, 37*(2), 135-140.

Walker, M. B. & Andrade, M. G. (1996). Conformity in the Asch task as a function of age. *Journal of Social Psychology, 136*(3), 367-372. doi:10.1080/00224545.1996.9714014

Context-dependent memory

Aslan, A., Samenieh, A., Staudigl, T., & Bäuml, K. T. (2010). Memorial consequences of environmental context change in children and adults. *Experimental Psychology, 57*(6), 455-461. doi:10.1027/1618-3169/a000056

Cairney, S. A., Durrant, S. J., Musgrove, H., & Lewis, P. A. (2011). Sleep and environmental context: Interactive effects for memory. *Experimental Brain Research, 214*(1), 83-92.

Debeer, E., Raes, F., Williams, J. M., & Hermans, D. (2011). Context-dependent activation of reduced autobiographical memory specificity as an avoidant coping style. *Emotion, 11*(6), 1500-1506.

Godden, D. R., & Baddeley, A. D. (1975). Context-dependent memory in two natural environments: On land and under water. *British Journal of Psychology, 66*(3), 325–331.

Goodwin, D., Powell, B., Bremer, D., Hoine, H., & Stern, J. (1969). Alcohol and recall: State-dependent effects in man. *Science, 163*(3873), 1358–1360.

Maren, S., Phan, K. L., & Liberzon, I. (2013). The contextual brain: Implications for fear conditioning, extinction, and psychopathology. *Nature Reviews Neuroscience, 14*(6), 417–428.

Marian, V., & Fausey, C. M. (2006). Language-dependent memory in bilingual learning. *Applied Cognitive Psychology, 20*, 1025-1047. doi: 10.1002/acp.1242

Marian, V., & Neisser, U. (2000). Language-dependent recall of autobiographical memories. *Journal of Experimental Psychology: General, 129*(3), 361–368.

Markopoulos, G., Rutherford, A., Cairns, C., & Green, J. (2010). Encoding instructions and stimulus presentation in local environmental context-dependent memory studies. *Memory, 18*(6), 610-624. doi: 10.1080/09658211.2010.497764

Masicampo, E. J., & Sahakyan, L. (2014). Imagining another context during encoding offsets context-dependent forgetting. *Journal of Experimental Psychology: Learning, Memory, and Cognition, 40*(6), 1772-1777. doi:10.1037/xlm0000007

McDaniel, M. A., & Einstein, G. O. (2007). *Prospective memory : An overview and synthesis of an emerging field.* Thousand Oaks, CA: SAGE Publications.

Murnane, K., Phelps, M. P., & Malmberg, K. (1999). Context-dependent recognition memory: The ICE theory. *Journal of Experimental Psychology: General, 128*(4), 403-415.

Pointer, S. C., & Bond, N. W. (1998). Context-dependent memory: Colour versus odor. *Chemical Senses, 23*(3), 359-362. doi:10.1093/chemse/23.3.359

Schwabe, L., Böhringer, A., & Wolf, O. T. (2009). Stress disrupts context-dependent memory. *Learning & Memory, 16*(2), 110-113. doi:10.1101/lm.1257509

Smith, S. M. (1988) Environmental context-dependent memory. In G. Davies (Ed.), *Memory in context* (pp. 13-31). Hoboken, NJ: Wiley.

Smith, S. M., & Vela, E. (2001). Environmental context-dependent memory: A review and meta-analysis. *Psychonomic Bulletin & Review, 8*(2), 203-220.

Exercise and depression

Blumenthal, J., Babyak, M., Doraiswamy, P., Watkins, L., Hoffman, B., Barbour, K., ... Sherwood, A. (2007). Exercise and pharmacotherapy in the treatment of major depressive disorder. *Psychosomatic Medicine, 69*(7), 587-596.

Daley, A. (2008). Exercise and depression: A review of reviews. *Journal of Clinical Psychology in Medical Settings, 15*(2), 140-147. doi:10.1007/s10880-008-9105-z

Dunn, A. L., Trivedi, M. H., Kampert, J. B., Clark, C. G., & Chambliss, H.O. (2005). Exercise treatment for depression: Efficacy and dose response. *American Journal of Preventive Medicine, 28*(1), 1-8.

Harris, D. V. (1987). Comparative effectiveness of running therapy and psychotherapy. In W. P. Morgan & S. E. Goldston (Eds.), *Exercise and mental health* (pp. 123-130). Washington, DC: Hemisphere Publishing Corp.

Jerstad, S. J., Boutelle, K. N., Ness, K. K., & Stice, E. (2010). Prospective reciprocal relations between physical activity and depression in female adolescents. *Journal of Consulting and Clinical Psychology, 78*(2), 268-272. doi:10.1037/a0018793

Martinsen, E. W., Medhus, A., & Sandvik, L. (1985). Effects of aerobic exercise of depression: A controlled study. *British Medical Journal, 291*(6488), 109.

Otto, M. W., & Smits, J. J. (2011). *Exercise for mood and anxiety: Proven strategies for overcoming depression and enhancing well-being.* New York, NY: Oxford University Press.

Rethorst, C. D., Toups, M. S., Greer, T. L., Nakonezny, P. A., Carmody, T. J., Grannemann, B. D., ... Trivedi, M. H. (2013). Pro-inflammatory cytokines as predictors of antidepressant effects of exercise in major depressive disorder. *Molecular Psychiatry, 18*(10), 1119-1124. doi:10.1038/mp.2012.125

Smits, J., Berry, A., Rosenfield, D., Powers, M., Behar, E., & Otto, M. (2008). Reducing anxiety sensitivity with exercise. *Depression and Anxiety, 25*, 689-699.

Stathopoulou, G., Powers, M. B., Berry, A. C., Smits, J. J., & Otto, M. W. (2006). Exercise interventions for mental health: A quantitative and qualitative review. *Clinical Psychology: Science and Practice, 13*(2), 179-193. doi:10.1111/j.1468-2850.2006.00021.x

Van de Vliet, P., Onghena, P., Knapen, J., Fox, K. R., Probst, M., Van Coppenolle, H., & Pieters, G. (2003). Assessing the additional impact of fitness training in depressed psychiatric patients receiving multifaceted treatment: A replicated single-subject design. *Disability and Rehabilitation: An International, Multidisciplinary Journal, 25*(24), 1344-1353. doi:10.1080/0963828031000I616330

Weinstein, A. A., Deuster, P. A., Francis, J. L., Beadling, C., & Kop, W. J. (2010). The role of depression in short-term mood and fatigue responses to acute exercise. *International Journal of Behavioral Medicine, 17*(1), 51-57. doi:10.1007/s12529-009-9046-4

Eyewitness testimony

Akehurst, L., Burden, N., & Buckle, J. (2009). Effect of socially encountered misinformation and delay on children's eyewitness testimony. *Psychiatry, Psychology and Law, 16*(1), S125-S136. doi:10.1080/13218710802620406

Coxon, P., & Valentine, T. (1997). The effects of the age of eyewitnesses on the accuracy and suggestibility of their testimony. *Applied Cognitive Psychology, 11*(5), 415-430.

Douglass, A. B., & Steblay, N. (2006). Memory distortion in eyewitnesses: A meta-analysis of the post-identification feedback effect. *Applied Cognitive Psychology, 20*(7), 859-869. doi:10.1002/acp.1237

Gurney, D. J., Pine, K. J., & Wiseman, R. (2013). The gestural misinformation effect: Skewing eyewitness testimony through gesture. *The American Journal of Psychology, 126*(3), 301-314.

Krähenbühl, S., Blades, M., & Eiser, C. (2009). The effect of repeated questioning on children's accuracy and consistency in eyewitness testimony. *Legal and Criminological Psychology, 14*(2), 263-278. doi:10.1348/135532508X398549

Lefebvre, C. D., Marchand, Y., Smith, S. M., & Connolly, J. F. (2007). Determining eyewitness identification accuracy using event-related brain potentials (ERPs). *Psychophysiology, 44*(6), 894-904. doi:10.1111/j.1469-8986.2007.00566.x

Lindsay, R. L., Ross, D. F., Read, J. D., & Toglia, M. P. (2007). *The handbook of eyewitness psychology, Vol II: Memory for people.* Mahwah, NJ: Lawrence Erlbaum Associates Publishers.

Loftus, E. F. (2013). Eyewitness testimony in the Lockerbie bombing case. *Memory, 21*(5), 584-590. doi:10.1080/09658211.2013.774417

Paz-Alonso, P. M., Goodman, G. S., & Ibabe, I. (2013). Adult eyewitness memory and compliance: Effects of post-event misinformation on memory for a negative event. *Behavioral Sciences & the Law, 31*(5), 541-558. doi:10.1002/bsl.2081

Toglia, M. P., Read, J. D., Ross, D. F., & Lindsay, R. L. (2007). *The handbook of eyewitness psychology, Vol I: Memory for events.* Mahwah, NJ: Lawrence Erlbaum Associates Publishers.

Valentine, T., & Maras, K. (2011). The effect of cross-examination on the accuracy of adult eyewitness testimony. *Applied Cognitive Psychology, 25*(4), 554-561. doi:10.1002/acp.1768

Wells, G. L., & Olson, E. A. (2003). Eyewitness testimony. *Annual Review of Psychology, 54*, 277-295. doi:10.1146/annurev.psych.54.101601.145028

Zember, E., Brainerd, C. J., Reyna, V. F., & Kopko, K. A. (2012). The science of law and memory. In E. Wethington & R. E. Dunifon (Eds.), *Research for the public good: Applying the methods of translational research to improve human health and well-being* (pp. 147-167). Washington, DC: American Psychological Association. doi:10.1037/13744-007

Mnemonics

Bellezza, F. S. (1987). Mnemonic devices and memory schemas. In M. A. McDaniel & M. Pressley (Eds.), *Imagery and related mnemonic processes* (pp. 34-55). New York, NY: Springer.

Bellezza, F. S. (1996). Mnemonic methods to enhance storage and retrieval. In E. L. Bjork & R. A. Bjork (Eds.), *Handbook of perception and cognition: Memory* (2nd ed., pp. 345-380). New York, NY: Academic Press.

Carney, R. N., & Levin, J. R. (2011). Delayed mnemonic benefits for a combined pegword-keyword strategy, time after time, rhyme after rhyme. *Applied Cognitive Psychology, 25*(2), 204-211.

Duffy, T. M., & Kearn, D. (1973). Mnemonics and intralist interference: A reexamination. *The American Journal of Psychology, 8*(4), 749-755.

Gardiner, J. C., & Thaut, M. H. (2014). Musical mnemonics training (MMT). In M. H. Thaut, V. Hoemberg, M. H. Thaut, & V. Hoemberg (Eds.), *Handbook of neurologic music therapy* (pp. 294-310). New York, NY: Oxford University Press.

Hall, C., Kent, S. C., McCulley, L., Davis, A., & Wanzek, J. (2013). A new look at mnemonics and graphic organizers in the secondary social studies classroom. *Teaching Exceptional Children, 46*(1), 47-55.

Leal, S. L., & Yassa, M. A. (2014). Effects of aging on mnemonic discrimination of emotional information. *Behavioral Neuroscience, 128*(5), 539-547. doi:10.1037/bne0000011

Mastropieri, M. A., Scruggs, T. E., & Levin, J. R. (1985). Maximizing what exceptional students can learn: A review of research on the keyword method and related mnemonic techniques. *RASE: Remedial & Special Education, 6*(2), 39-45. doi:10.1177/074193258500600208

Mastropieri, M. A., Scruggs, T. E., & Whedon, C. (1997). Using mnemonic strategies to teach information about U.S. Presidents: A classroom-based investigation. *Learning Disability Quarterly, 20*(1), 13-21. doi:10.2307/1511089

Verhaeghen, P., Marcoen, A., & Goossens, L. (1992). Improving memory performance in the aged through mnemonic training: A meta-analytic study. *Psychology and Aging, 7*(2), 242-251. doi:10.1037/0882-7974.7.2.242

Worthen, J. B., & Hunt, R. R. (2011). *Mnemonology: Mnemonics for the 21st century.* New York, NY: Psychology Press.

Mood and recall

Blaney, P. H. (1986). Affect and memory: A review. *Psychological Bulletin, 99*(2), 229-246. doi:10.1037/0033-2909.99.2.229
Bower, G. (1981). Mood and memory under natural conditions: Evidence for mood incongruent recall. *American Psychologist, 36*(2), 129-148.
Corson, Y., & Verrier, N. (2007). Emotions and false memories: Valence or arousal? *Psychological Science, 18*(3), 208-211.
Erber, R., & Wang-Erber, M. (1993). Beyond mood and social judgement: Mood incongruent recall and mood regulation. *European Journal of Social Psychology, 24*, 79-88.
Guenther, K. (1988). Mood and memory. In G. M. Davies & D. M. Thomson (Eds.), *Memory in context: Context in memory* (pp. 58-75). Chichester, UK: Wiley.
Lee, A., & Sternthal, B. (1999). The effects of positive mood on memory. *Journal of Consumer Research, 26*, 115-127.
Levy, E. A., & Mineka, S. (1998). Anxiety and mood-congruent autobiographical memory: A conceptual failure to replicate. *Cognition and Emotion, 12*(5), 625-634. doi:10.1080/026999398379475
Martin, L. L., & Clore, G. L. (2001). *Theories of mood and cognition: A user's guidebook.* Mahwah, NJ: Lawrence Erlbaum Associates Publishers.
Matt, G. E., Vázquez, C., & Campbell, W. K. (1992). Mood-congruent recall of affectively toned stimuli: A meta-analytic review. *Clinical Psychology Review, 12*(2), 227-255.
Munger, D. (2009, September 8). Memory and mood: Negative emotions nullify a problem with recall. *Science Blogs.* Retrieved from http://scienceblogs.com/
Parrott, W. G., & Sabini, J. (1990). Mood and memory under natural conditions: Evidence for mood incongruent recall. *Journal of Personality and Social Psychology, 59*(2), 321-336. doi:10.1037/0022-3514.59.2.321
Ramponi, C., Barnard, P. J., & Nimmo-Smith, I. (2004). Recollection deficits in dysphoric mood: An effect of schematic models and executive mode?. *Memory, 12*(5), 655-670. doi:10.1080/09658210344000189
Sakaki, M. (2004). Effects of self-complexity on mood-incongruent recall. *Japanese Psychological Research, 46*(2), 127-134. doi:10.1111/j.0021-5368.2004.00244.x
Storbeck, J., & Clore, G. (2005). With sadness comes accuracy; With happiness, false memory. Mood and the false memory effect. *Psychological Science, 16*(10), 785-791. doi: 10.1111/j.1467-9280.2005.01615.x

Müller-Lyer illusion

Brosvic, G. M., Dihoff, R. E., & Fama, J. (2002). Age-related susceptibility to the Müller-Lyer and the Horizontal-Vertical illusions. *Perceptual and Motor Skills, 94*(1), 229-234. doi:10.2466/PMS.94.1.229-234

Bruno, N., & Franz, V. H. (2009). When is grasping affected by the Müller-Lyer illusion? A quantitative review. *Neuropsychologia, 47*(6), 1421-1433.

Day, R. (2010). On the common stimulus condition and explanation of the Müller-Lyer, Poggendorff and Zöllner illusions: The basis for a class of geometrical illusions. *Australian Journal of Psychology, 62*(3), 115-120. doi:10.1080/00049530903510773

Gillan, D. J., Schmidt, W., & Hanowski, R. J. (1999). The effect of the Müller-Lyer illusion on map reading. *Perception & Psychophysics, 61*(6), 1154-1167. doi:10.3758/BF03207620

Hamilton, V. (1966). Susceptibility to the Müller-Lyer illusion and its relationship to differences in size constancy. *The Quarterly Journal of Experimental Psychology, 18*(1), 63-72. doi:10.1080/14640746608400008

Howe, C., & Purves, D. (2005). The Müller-Lyer Illusion explained by the statistics of image-source relationships. *Proceedings of the National Academy of Sciences of the United States of America, 102*(4), 1234-1239.

Koch, C., & Hayworth, E. S. (2003). Examining the relationship between need for cognition and the Muller-Lyer illusion. *North American Journal of Psychology, 5*(2), 249-255.

McCauley, R. N., & Henrich, J. (2006). Susceptibility to the Müller-Lyer illusion, theory-neutral observation, and the diachronic penetrability of the visual input system. *Philosophical Psychology, 19*(1), 79-101. doi:10.1080/09515080500462347

Millar, S., & Al-Attar, Z. (2002). The Müller-Lyer illusion in touch and vision: Implications for multisensory processes. *Perception & Psychophysics, 64*(3), 353-365. doi:10.3758/BF03194709

Mundy, M. E. (2014). Testing day: The effects of processing bias induced by Navon stimuli on the strength of the Müller-Lyer illusion. *Advances in Cognitive Psychology, 10*(1), 9-14.doi: 10.2478/v10053-008-0151-8

Nijhawan, R. (1997). The Müller-Lyer illusion re-examined. In I. Rock (Ed.), *Indirect perception* (pp. 315-3333). Cambridge, MA: MIT Press.

Pinter, R., & Anderson, M. M. (1916). The Müller-Lyer illusion with children and adults. *Journal of Experimental Psychology, 1*(3), 200-210. doi:10.1037/h0074617

Predebon, J. (2000). Length illusions in conventional and single-wing Müller-Lyer stimuli. *Perception & Psychophysics, 62*(5), 1086-1098. doi:10.3758/BF03212090

Schiano, D. J., & Jordan, K. (1990). Mueller-Lyer decrement: Practice or prolonged inspection? *Perception, 19*(3), 307-316. doi:10.1068/p190307

Naps and memory consolidation

Alger, S. E., Lau, H., & Fishbein, W. (2010). Delayed onset of a daytime nap facilitates retention of declarative memory. *Plos ONE, 5*(8), 1-9. doi:10.1371/journal.pone.0012131

Helm, E. D., Gujar, N., Nishida, M., & Walker, M. P. (2011). Sleep-dependent facilitation of episodic memory details. *Plos ONE, 6*(11), 1-10. doi:10.1371/journal.pone.0027421

Hiuyan, L., Alger, S. E., & Fishbein, W. (2011). Relational memory: A daytime nap facilitates the abstraction of general concepts. *Plos ONE, 6*(11), 1-6. doi:10.1371/journal.pone.0027139

Karbach, J., & Verhaeghen, P. (2014). Making working memory work: A meta-analysis of executive-control and working memory training in older adults. *Psychological Science, 25*(11), 2027-2037. doi:10.1177/0956797614548725

Kurdziel, L., Duclos, K., & Spencer, R. C. (2013). Sleep spindles in midday naps enhance learning in preschool children. *Proceedings of the National Academy of Sciences of the United States of America, 110*(43), 17267-17272. doi:10.1073/pnas.1306418110

Lemos, N., Weissheimer, J., & Ribeiro, S. (2014). Naps in school can enhance the duration of declarative memories learned by adolescents. *Frontiers in Systems Neuroscience, 8*, 103.

Lo, J. C., Dijk, D., & Groeger, J. A. (2014). Comparing the effects of nocturnal sleep and daytime napping on declarative memory consolidation. *Plos ONE, 9*(9), 1-5. doi:10.1371/journal.pone.0108100

Nalbantian, S., Matthews, P., & McClelland, J. (2011). *The memory process neuroscientific and humanistic perspectives.* Cambridge, MA: MIT Press.

Nishida, M., & Walker, M. P. (2007). Daytime naps, motor memory consolidation and regionally specific sleep spindles. *Plos ONE, 2*(4), e341.

Pöllänen, S. H., & Hirsimäki, R. M. (2014). Crafts as memory triggers in reminiscence: A case study of older women with dementia. *Occupational Therapy in Health Care, 28*(4), 410-430. doi:10.3109/07380577.2014.941052

Stickgold, R. (2005). Sleep-dependent memory consolidation. *Nature, 437*(7063), 1272-1278. doi:10.1038/nature04286

Takashima, A., Petersson, K. M., Rutters, F., Tendolkar, I., Jensen, O., Zwarts, M. J., . . . Fernández, G. (2006). Declarative memory consolidation in humans: A prospective functional magnetic resonance imaging study. *Proceedings of the National Academy of Sciences of the United States of America, 103*(3), 756-761. doi:10.1073/pnas.0507774103

Tietzel, A. J., & Lack, L. C. (2002). The recuperative value of brief and ultra-brief naps on alertness and cognitive performance. *Journal of Sleep Research, 11*(3), 213-218. doi:10.1046/j.1365-2869.2002.00299.x

Walker, M. R. (2005). A refined model of sleep and the time course of memory formation. *Behavioral & Brain Sciences, 28*(1), 51-64.

Placebo effect

Benedetti, F., Mayberg, H. S., Wager, T. D., Stohler, C. S., & Zubieta, J. (2005). Neurobiological mechanisms of the placebo effect. *The Journal of Neuroscience, 25*(45), 10390-10402.

Bolton, P., Shotton, L., Young, A., & Grace, J. (2012). The ethics of using placebo medication in a non-capacitous patient. *Brain Injury, 26*(11), 1397-1400. doi:10.3109/02699052.2012.694560

Brody, H., Colloca, L., & Miller, F. (2012). The placebo phenomenon: Implications for the ethics of shared decision-making. *Journal of General Internal Medicine, 27*(6), 739-742. doi:10.1007/s11606-011-1977-1

Faria, V., Fredrikson, M., & Furmark, T. (2008). Imaging the placebo response: A neurofunctional review. *European Neuropsychopharmacology, 18*(7), 473-485. doi:10.1016/j.euroneuro.2008.03.002

Harrington, A. (1999). *The placebo effect: An interdisciplinary exploration.* Cambridge, MA: Harvard University Press.

Johnson, H. H., & Foley, J. M. (1969). Some effects of placebo and experiment conditions in research on methods of teaching. *Journal of Educational Psychology, 60*(1), 6-10.

Kaptchuk, T. J., Friedlander, E., Kelley, J. M., Sanchez, M., Kokkotou, E., Singer, J. P., ... Lembo, A. J. (2010). Placebos without deception: A randomized controlled trial in irritable bowel syndrome. *Plos ONE, 5*(12), 1-7. doi:10.1371/journal.pone.0015591

Kirsch, I. (2014) Antidepressants and the placebo effect. *Zeitschrift Für Psychologie, 222*(3), 128-134.

Mayberg, H. S., Silva, A. J., Brannan, S. K., Tekell, J. L., Mahurin, R. K., McGinnis, S., & Jerabek, P. A. (2012). The functional neuroanatomy of the placebo effect. *American Journal of Psychiatry, 159*(5), 728-737.

Miller, F. G., & Brody, H. (2011). Understanding and harnessing placebo effects: Clearing away the underbrush. *Journal of Medicine & Philosophy, 36*(1), 69-78. doi:10.1093/jmp/jhq061

Moerman, D. E. (2002). *Meaning, medicine, and the placebo effect.* New York, NY: Press Syndicate of the University of Cambridge.

Price, D. D., Milling L. S., Kirsch, I., Duff, A., Montgomery, G. H., & Nicholls, S. S. (1999). An analysis of factors that contribute to the magnitude of placebo analgesia in an experimental paradigm. *Pain, 8*(3), 147-156.

Streitberger, K., & Kleinhenz, J. (1998). Introducing a placebo needle into acupuncture research. *Lancet, 352*(9125), 364.

Sümegi, Z., Gácsi, M., & Topál, J. (2014). Conditioned placebo effect in dogs decreases separation related behaviours. *Applied Animal Behaviour Science, 159*, 90-98. doi:10.1016/j.applanim.2014.07.005

Vase, L., Skyt, I., Laue Petersen, G., & Price, D. D. (2014). Placebo and nocebo effects in chronic pain patients: How expectations and emotional feelings contribute to the experience of pain. *Zeitschrift Für Psychologie, 222*(3), 135-139.

Stroop effect

Brown, T. L., Joneleit, K., Robinson, C. S., & Brown, C. R. (2002). Automaticity in reading and the Stroop task: Testing the limits of involuntary word processing. *The American Journal of Psychology, 115*(4), 515-543.

MacLeod, C. M. (1991). Half a century of research on the Stroop effect: An integrative review. *Psychological Bulletin, 109*(2), 163-203. doi:10.1037/0033-2909.109.2.163

MacLeod, C. (2005). The Stroop task in clinical research. In A. Wenzel, D. C. Rubin, A. Wenzel, D. C. Rubin (Eds.), *Cognitive methods and their application to clinical research* (pp. 41-62). Washington, DC: American Psychological Association. doi:10.1037/10870-003

Mayor, J., Sainz, J., & Gonzalez-Marques, J. (1988). Stroop and priming effects in naming and categorizing tasks using words and pictures. In M. Denis, J. Engelkamp, J. E. Richardson, M. Denis, J. Engelkamp, J. E. Richardson (Eds.), *Cognitive and neuropsychological approaches to mental imagery* (pp. 69-78). Dordrecht, Netherlands: Martinus Nijhoff Publishing.

Navarrete, E., Sessa, P., Peressotti, F., & Dell'Acqua, R. (2015). The distractor frequency effect in the colour-naming Stroop task: An overt naming event-related potential study. *Journal of Cognitive Psychology, 27*(3), 277-289. doi:10.1080/20445911.2014.1002786

Prevor, M. B., & Diamond, A. (2005). Color-object interference in young children: A Stroop effect in children 3½-6½ years old. *Cognitive Development, 20*(2), 256-278.

Raz, A., Kirsch, I., Pollard, J., & Nitkin-Kaner, Y. (2006). Suggestion reduces the Stroop effect. *Psychological Science, 17*(2), 91-95.

Sheehan, P. W., Donovan, P., & MacLeod, C. M. (1988). Strategy manipulation and the Stroop effect in hypnosis. *Journal of Abnormal Psychology, 97*(4), 455-460. doi:10.1037/0021-843X.97.4.455

Tzelgov, J., Porat, Z., & Henik, A. (1997). Automaticity and consciousness: Is perceiving the word necessary for reading it? *The American Journal of Psychology, 110*(3), 429-448.

Verhaeghen, P., & De Meersman, L. (1998). Aging and the Stroop effect: A meta-analysis. *Psychology and Aging, 13*(1), 120-126. doi: 10.1037/0882-7974.13.1.120

Washburn, D. A. (1994). Stroop-like effects for monkeys and humans: Processing speed or strength of association? *Psychological Science, 5*(6), 375-379.

Treatment of ADHD

Bailey, U. L., Derefinko, K. J., Milich, R., Lorch, E. P., & Metze, A. (2011). The effects of stimulant medication on free recall of story events among children with ADHD. *Journal of Psychopathology and Behavioral Assessment, 33*(4), 409-419.

Cortese, S., Holtmann, M., Banaschewski, T., Buitelaar, J., Coghill, D., Danckaerts, M., ... Sergeant, J. (2013). Practitioner review: Current best practice in the management of adverse events during treatment with ADHD medications in children and adolescents. *Journal of Child Psychology & Psychiatry, 54*(3), 227-246. doi:10.1111/jcpp.12036

Greydanus, D. (2005). Pharmacologic treatment of attention-deficit hyperactivity disorder. *The Indian Journal of Pediatrics, 72*(11), 953-960.

Groen, Y., Gaastra, G. F., Lewis-Evans, B., & Tucha, O. (2013). Risky behavior in gambling tasks in individuals with ADHD—A systematic literature review. *Plos ONE, 8*(9), e74909. doi:10.1371/journal.pone.0074909

Halldner, L., Tillander, A., Lundholm, C., Boman, M., Långström, N., Larsson, H., & Lichtenstein, P. (2014). Relative immaturity and ADHD: Findings from nationwide registers, parent- and self-reports. *Journal of Child Psychology and Psychiatry, 55*(8), 897-904. doi:10.1111/jcpp.12229

Meaux, J. B. (2000). Stop, look, and listen: The challenge for children with ADHD. *Issues in Comprehensive Pediatric Nursing, 23*(1), 1-13. doi:10.1080/01460860050121394

Mowinckel, A. M., Pedersen, M. L., Eilertsen, E., & Biele, G. (2015). A meta-analysis of decision-making and attention in adults with ADHD. *Journal of Attention Disorders, 19*(5), 355-367. doi:10.1177/1087054714558872

Nikkelen, S. C., Valkenburg, P. M., Huizinga, M., & Bushman, B. J. (2014). Media use and ADHD-related behaviors in children and adolescents: A meta-analysis. *Developmental Psychology, 50*(9), 2228-2241. doi:10.1037/a0037318

Rucklidge, J. J., & Harrison, R. (2010). Successful treatment of bipolar disorder II and ADHD with a micronutrient formula: A case study. *CNS Spectrums, 15*(5), 289-295.

Selikowitz, M. (2009). *ADHD* (2nd ed.). Oxford, UK: Oxford University Press.

Sumner, C., Gathercole, S., Greenbaum, M., Rubin, R., Williams, D., Hollandbeck, M., & Wietecha, L. (2009). Atomoxetine For The Treatment Of Attention-Deficit/ Hyperactivity Disorder (ADHD) In Children With ADHD And Dyslexia. *Child and Adolescent Psychiatry and Mental Health, 3*,40. doi:10.1186/1753-2000-3-40

Surman, C. H., Hammerness, P. G., Pion, K., & Faraone, S. V. (2013). Do stimulants improve functioning in adults with ADHD?: A review of the literature. *European Neuropsychopharmacology, 23*(6), 528-533. doi:10.1016/j.euroneuro.2012.02.010

Treatment of Alzheimer's Disease

Assal, F. (2011). Neuropsychiatric treatments in Alzheimer's disease. In P. McNamara, P. McNamara (Eds.), *Dementia, Vols 1–3: History and incidence, Science and biology, Treatments and developments* (pp. 205-231). Santa Barbara, CA: Praeger/ABC-CLIO.

Dodd, K. (2010). Psychological and other non-pharmacological interventions in services for people with learning disabilities and dementia. *Advances in Mental Health and Learning Disabilities, 4*(1), 28-35. doi: 10.5042/amhld.2010.0056

Fukui, H. H., Arai, A. A., & Toyoshima, K. K. (2012). Efficacy of music therapy in treatment for the patients with Alzheimer's Disease. *International Journal of Alzheimer's Disease*, 1-6. doi:10.1155/2012/531646

Götell, E., Brown, S., & Ekman, S. (2009). The influence of caregiver singing and background music on vocally expressed emotions and moods in dementia care: A qualitative analysis. *International Journal of Nursing Studies, 46*(4), 422–430. doi: 10.1016/j.ijnurstu.2007.11.001

Guétin, S. S., Portet, F. F., Picot, M. C., Pommié, C. C., Messaoudi, M. M., Djabelkir, L. L., ... Touchon, J. J. (2009). Effect of music therapy on anxiety and depression in patients with Alzheimer's type dementia: Randomised, controlled study. *Dementia & Geriatric Cognitive Disorders, 28*(1), 36-46. doi:10.1159/000229024

Katz, I., De Deyn, P., Mintzer, J., Greenspan, A., Zhu, Y., & Brodaty, H. (2007). The efficacy and safety of Risperidone in the treatment of psychosis of Alzheimer's disease: A meta-analysis of 4 placebo-controlled clinical trials. *International Journal of Geriatric Psychiatry, 22*(5), 475-484. doi: 10.1002/gps.1792

Ledger, A. J., & Baker, F. A. (2007). An investigation of long-term effects of group music therapy on agitation levels of people with Alzheimer's Disease. *Aging & Mental Health, 11*(3), 330-338. doi:10.1080/13607860600963406

Li, M., Guo, K., & Ikehara, S. (2014). Stem cell treatment for Alzheimer's Disease. *International Journal of Molecular Sciences, 15*(10), 19226-19238. doi: 10.3390/ijms151019226

Lu, L. C., & Bludau, J. (2011). *Alzheimer's disease*. Santa Barbara, CA: Greenwood Publishing Group.

Lyubartseva, G., & Lovell, M. A. (2012). A potential role for zinc alterations in the pathogenesis of Alzheimer's disease. *Biofactors, 38*(2), 98-106. doi: 10.1002/biof.199

Hogan, D. B., (2014). Long-term efficacy and toxicity of cholinesterase inhibitors in the treatment of Alzheimer Disease. *Canadian Journal of Psychiatry, 59*(12), 618-623.

Robinson, P., Giorgi, B., & Ekman, S. (2012). The lived experience of early stage Alzheimer's Disease: A three-year longitudinal phenomenological case study. *Journal of Phenomenological Psychology, 43*(2), 216-238. doi: 10.1163/15691624-12341236

Treatment of Bipolar disorder

Benazzi, F. (1997). Prevalence of bipolar II disorder in outpatient depression: A 203-case study in private practice. *Journal of Affective Disorders, 43*(2), 163-166. doi:10.1016/S0165-0327(96)01421-8

Calabrese, J. R., Keck, P. E., Macfadden, W., Minkwitz, M., Ketter, T. A., Weisler, R. H., ... Mullen, J. (2005). A randomized, double-blind, placebo-controlled trial of quetiapine in the treatment of bipolar I or II depression. *American Journal of Psychiatry, 162*(7), 1351-1360.

Dinan, T. G. (2002). Lithium in bipolar mood disorder. *BMJ, 324*, 989-990.

Geddes, J. R., Burgess, S., Hawton, K., Jamison, K., & Goodwin, G. M. (2004). Long-term lithium therapy for bipolar disorder: Systematic review and meta-analysis of randomized controlled trials. *American Journal of Psychiatry, 161*(2), 217-222.

Goodwin, G. M., Bowden, C. L., Calabrese, J. R., Grunze, H., Kasper, S., White, R., ... Leadbetter, R. (2004). A pooled analysis of 2 placebo-controlled 18-month trials of lamotrigine and lithium maintenance in bipolar I disorder. *Journal of Clinical Psychiatry, 65*, 432-441.

Guzzetta, F., Tondo, L., Centorrino, F., & Baldessarini, R. J. (2007). Lithium treatment reduces suicide risk in recurrent major depressive disorder. *Journal of Clinical Psychology, 683*, 380-383.

Mostafavi, A., Solhi, M., Mohammadi, M. R., Hamedi, M., Keshavarzi, M., & Akhondzadeh, S. (2014). Melatonin decreases Olanzapine induced metabolic side-effects in adolescents with bipolar disorder: A randomized double-blind placebo-controlled trial. *Acta Medica Iranica, 52*(10), 734-739.

Olvet, D. M., Burdick, K. E., & Cornblatt, B. A. (2013). Assessing the potential to use neurocognition to predict who is at risk for developing bipolar disorder: A review of the literature. *Cognitive Neuropsychiatry, 18*, 129-145. doi:10.1080/13546805.2012.724193

Oquendo, M. A., Galfalvy, H. C., Currier, D., Grunebaum, M. F., Sher, L., Sullivan, G. M., ... Mann, J. J. (2011). Treatment of suicide attempters with bipolar disorder: A randomized clinical trial comparing lithium and valporate in the prevention of suicidal behavior. *American Journal of Psychiatry, 168*, 1050-1056. doi:10.1176/appi.ajp.2011.11010163

Perry, A., Tarrier, N., Morriss, R., McCarthy, E., & Limb, K. (1999). Randomised controlled trial of efficacy of teaching patients with bipolar disorder to identify early symptoms of relapse and obtain treatment. *BMJ, 318*, 149-153.

Plunkett, J. M. (2011). *Bipolar disorder: Causes, diagnosis and treatment.* New York, NY: Nova Science Publishers.

Schou, M., Juel-Nielsen, N., Stromgren, E., & Voldby, H. (1954). The treatment of manic psychoses by the administration of lithium salts. *Journal of Neurological Neurosurgical Psychiatry, 17*, 250–260.

Sung, T., Chen, M., & Su, H. (2013). A positive relationship between ambient temperature and bipolar disorder identified using a national cohort of psychiatric inpatients. *Social Psychiatry & Psychiatric Epidemiology, 48*(2), 295-302.

Treatment of Depression

Beck, A. T., Rush, J. A., Shaw, B. F., & Emery, G. (1979). *Cognitive therapy of depression*. New York, NY: The Guilford Press.

Bowers, W. A. (1990). Treatment of depressed in-patients. Cognitive therapy plus medication, relaxation plus medication, and medication alone. *British Journal of Psychiatry, 156*(1), 73-78.

Butler, A. C., Chapman, J. E., Forman, E. M., & Beck, A. T. (2006). The empirical status of cognitive-behavioral therapy: A review of meta-analyses. *Clinical Psychology Review, 26*(1), 17-31. doi:10.1016/j.cpr.2005.07.003

Cipriani, A. (2009). Comparative efficacy and acceptability of 12 new-generation antidepressants: A multiple-treatments meta-analysis. *The Lancet, 373*(9665), 746-758.

Clayton, P. J., & Barrett, J. E. (1983). *Treatment of depression: Old controversies and new approaches*. New York, NY: Raven Press Books.

Cuijpers, P., Straten, A. V., & Warmerdam, L. (2006). Behavioral activation treatments of depression: A meta-analysis. *Clinical Psychology Review, 27*(3), 318-326.

Driessen, E., Van, H. L., Don, F. J., Peen, J., Kool, S., Westra, D., ... Dekker, J. M. (2013). The efficacy of cognitive-behavioral therapy and psychodynamic therapy in the outpatient treatment of major depression: A randomized clinical trial. *The American Journal of Psychiatry, 170*(9), 1041-1050. doi:10.1176/appi.ajp.2013.12070899

Fournier, J. C., DeRubeis, R. J., Shelton, R. C., Hollon, S. D., Amsterdam, J. D., & Gallop, R. (2009). Prediction of response to medication and cognitive therapy in the treatment of moderate to severe depression. *Journal of Consulting Psychology, 77*(4), 775-787.

Healy, D. (1997). *The antidepressant era*. Cambridge, MA: Harvard University Press.

Jacobson, N. S., Martell, C. R., & Dimidjian, S. (2006). Behavioral activation treatment for depression: Returning to contextual roots. *Clinical Psychology: Science and Practice, 8*(3), 255-270.

Khalsa, S., McCarthy, K. S., Sharpless, B. A., Barrett, M. S., & Barber, J. P. (2011). Beliefs about the causes of depression and treatment preferences. *Journal of Clinical Psychology, 67*(6), 539-549. doi:10.1002/jclp.20785

Lanzenberger, R., Baldinger, P., Hahn, A., Ungersboeck, J., Mitterhauser, M., Winkler, D., ... Frey, R. (2013). Global decrease of serotonin-1A receptor binding after electroconvulsive therapy in major depression measured by PET. *Molecular Psychiatry, 18*(1), 93-100. doi:10.1038/mp.2012.93

Rush, A. J., Beck, A. T., Kovacs, M., & Hollon, S. (1977). Comparative efficacy of cognitive therapy and imipramine in the treatment of depressed outpatients. *Cognitive Therapy and Research, 1*, 17-37.

Rush, A. J., Khatami, M., & Beck, A. T. (1975). Cognitive and behavioral therapy in chronic depression. *Behavior Therapy, 6*, 398-404.

Treatment of Obsessive Compulsive Disorder

Abramowitz, J. S. (1997). Effectiveness of psychological and pharmacological treatments for obsessive-compulsive disorder: A quantitative review. *Journal of Consulting and Clinical Psychology, 65*(1), 44-52.

Bengel, D., Greenberg, B. D., Cora-Locatelli, G., Altemus, M., Heils, A., Li, Q., & Murphy, D. L. (1999). Association of the serotonin transporter promoter regulatory region polymorphism and obsessive-compulsive disorder. *Molecular Psychiatry, 4*, 463-466.

Bolton, D., Williams, T., Perrin, S., Atkinson, L., Gallop, C., Waite, P., & Salkovskis, P. (2011). Randomized controlled trial of full and brief cognitive-behaviour therapy and wait-list for paediatric obsessive-compulsive disorder. *Journal of Child Psychology and Psychiatry, 52*(12), 1269-1278. doi:10.1111/j.1469-7610.2011.02419.x

Dembo, J. S. (2014). "The ickiness factor:" Case study of an unconventional psychotherapeutic approach to pediatric OCD. *American Journal of Psychotherapy, 68*(1), 57-79.

Foa, E. B., & Franklin, M. E. (2001). Obsessive-compulsive disorder. In D. H. Barlow (Ed.), *Clinical handbook of psychological disorders: A step-by-step treatment manual* (3rd ed.) (pp. 209-263). New York, NY: Guilford Press.

Freeman, J., Sapyta, J., Garcia, A., Fitzgerald, D., Khanna, M., Choate-Summers, M., ... Franklin, M. (2011). Still struggling: Characteristics of youth with OCD who are partial responders to medication treatment. *Child Psychiatry and Human Development, 42*(4), 424-441. doi:10.1007/s10578-011-0227-4

Geller, D., Biederman, L. J., Faraon, S. V., Frazier, J., Coffey, B. J., Kim, G., & Bellordre, C. A. (2000). Clinical correlates of obsessive compulsive disorder in children and adolescents referred to specialized and non-specialized clinical settings. *Depression & Anxiety, 11*(4), 163-168.

Pozza, A., Andersson, G., Antonelli, P., & Dèttore, D. (2014). Computer-delivered cognitive-behavioural treatments for obsessive compulsive disorder: Preliminary meta-analysis of randomized and non-randomized effectiveness trials. *The Cognitive Behaviour Therapist, 7*, e16. doi:10.1017/S1754470X1400021X

Renshaw, K. D., Steketee, G., & Chambless, D. L. (2005). Involving family members in the treatment of OCD. *Cognitive Behaviour Therapy, 34*(3), 164-175. doi:10.1080/16506070510043732

Sayyah, M., Sayyah, M., Boostani, H., Ghaffari, S. M., & Hoseini, A. (2012). Effects of aripiprazole augmentation in treatment-resistant obsessive-compulsive disorder (a double blind clinical trial). *Depression and Anxiety, 29*(10), 850-854. doi:10.1002/da.21996

Zohar, J. (2012). *Obsessive compulsive disorder: Current science and clinical practice.* Hoboken, NJ: Wiley-Blackwell. doi:10.1002/9781119941125

Treatment of Phobias

Botella, C., Breton-Lopez, J., Quero, S., Banos, R.M., Garcia-Palacios, A., Zaragoza, I., & Alcaniz, M. (2011). Treating cockroach phobia using a serious game on a mobile phone and augmented reality exposure: A single case study. *Computers in Human Behavior, 27*(1), 217-227.

Chou, K. L. (2009). Specific phobia in older adults: Evidence from the national epidemiological survey on alcohol and related conditions. *The American Journal of Geriatric Psychiatry, 17*(5), 376-386.

Cote, S., & Bouchard, S. (2008). Virtual reality exposures for phobias: A critical review. *Journal of CyberTherapy & Rehabilitation, 1*(1), 75-91.

Cox, R. P., & Howard, M. D. (2007). Utilization of EMDR in the treatment of sexual addiction: A case study. *Sexual Addiction & Compulsivity, 14*(1), 1-20. doi:10.1080/10720160601011299

Craske, M. G., Niles, A. N., Burklund, L. J., Wolitzky-Taylor, K. B., Vilardaga, J. P., Arch, J. J., ... Lieberman, M. D. (2014). Randomized controlled trial of cognitive behavioral therapy and acceptance and commitment therapy for social phobia: Outcomes and moderators. *Journal of Consulting and Clinical Psychology, 82*(6), 1034-1048. doi:10.1037/a0037212

Davis III, T. E., Ollendick, T. H., Ost, L. (Eds.) (2012). *Intensive one-session treatment of specific phobias*. New York, NY: Springer.

Harold, L., Agras, W. S., Robert, A., Robert, B., & Joyce, E. (1975). Feedback and therapist praise during treatment of phobia. *Journal of Consulting and Clinical Psychology, 43*(3), 396-404. doi:10.1037/h0076742

Hoffman, H. G., Garcia-Palacios, A., Carlin, A., Furness, T. I., & Botella-Arbona, C. (2003). Interfaces that heal: Coupling real and virtual objects to treat spider phobia. *International Journal of Human-Computer Interaction, 16*(2), 283-300. doi:10.1207/S15327590IJHC1602_08

Howard, M. D., & Cox, R. P. (2006). Use of EMDR in the treatment of water phobia at Navy boot camp: A case study. *Traumatology, 12*(4), 302-313. doi:10.1177/1534765606297821

Lazarus, A. A. (1961). Group therapy of phobic disorders by systematic desensitization. *The Journal of Abnormal and Social Psychology, 63*(3), 504-510.

Marks, I. (1987). *Fears, phobias and rituals: Panic, anxiety, and their disorders*. New York, NY: Oxford University Press.

Ollendick, T. H., Öst, L., Reuterskiöld, L., Costa, N., Cederlund, R., Sirbu, C., ... Jarrett, M. A. (2009). One-session treatment of specific phobias in youth: A randomized clinical trial in the United States and Sweden. *Journal of Consulting and Clinical Psychology, 77*(3), 504-516. doi:10.1037/a0015158

Taylor, S. (1996). Meta-analysis of cognitive-behavioral treatments for social phobia. *Journal of Behavior Therapy and Experimental Psychiatry, 27*(1), 1-9.

Watson, J. B., & Rayner, R. (1920). Conditioned emotional reactions. *Journal of Experimental Psychology, 3*(1), 1-14. doi:10.1037/h0069608

Treatment of Post-Traumatic Stress Disorder (PTSD)

Bernardy, N. C., & Friedman, M. J. (2015). *A practical guide to PTSD treatment: Pharmacological and psychotherapeutic approaches*. Washington, DC: American Psychological Association. doi:10.1037/14522-000

Bradley, R., Jamelle, G., Eric, R., Lissa, D., & Drew, W. (2005). A multidimensional meta-analysis of psychotherapy for PTSD. *American Journal of Psychiatry, 162*(2), 214-227.

Gonçalves, R., Pedrozo, A. L., Freire-Coutinho, E. S., Figueira, I., & Ventura, P. (2012). Efficacy of virtual reality exposure therapy in the treatment of PTSD: A systematic review. *Plos ONE, 7*(12), 1-7. doi:10.1371/journal.pone.0048469

Kozarić-Kovacić, D. (2009). Pharmacotherapy treatment of PTSD and comorbid disorders. *Psychiatria Danubina, 21*(3), 411-414.

Leard-Mann, C., Kelton, M., Smith, B., Littman, A., Boyko, E., Wells, T., & Smith, T. (2011). Prospectively assessed Posttraumatic Stress Disorder and associated physical activity. *Public Health Reports, 126*(3), 371-383.

McLay, R. N., Graap, K., Spira, J., Perlman, K., Johnston, S., Rothbaum, B. O., & Rizzo, A. (2012). Development and testing of virtual reality exposure therapy for Post-Traumatic Stress Disorder in active duty service members who served in Iraq and Afghanistan. *Military Medicine, 177*(6), 635-642.

Monson, C. M., & Shnaider, P. (2014). *Treating PTSD with cognitive-behavioral therapies: Interventions that work*. Washington, DC: American Psychological Association. doi:10.1037/14372-003

Pacella, M. L., Feeny, N., Zoellner, L., & Delahanty, D. L. (2014). The impact of PTSD treatment on the cortisol awakening response. *Depression and Anxiety, 31*(10), 862-869. doi:10.1002/da.22298

Rauch, S. A., Eftekhari, A., & Ruzek, J. I. (2012). Review of exposure therapy: A gold standard for PTSD treatment. *Journal of Rehabilitation Research & Development, 49*(5), 678-687. doi:10.1682/JRRD.2011.08.0152

Sloan, D. M., Lee, D. J., Litwack, S. D., Sawyer, A. T., & Marx, B. P. (2013). Written exposure therapy for veterans diagnosed with PTSD: A pilot study. *Journal of Traumatic Stress, 26*(6), 776-779. doi:10.1002/jts.21858

Stapleton, J. A., Taylor, S., & Asmundson, G. G. (2007). Efficacy of various treatments for PTSD in battered women: Case studies. *Journal of Cognitive Psychotherapy, 21*(1), 91-102. doi:10.1891/088983907780493287

Steckler, T., & Risbrough, V. (2012). Pharmacological treatment of PTSD – Established and new approaches. *Neuropharmacology, 62*(2), 617-627.

Sutherland, R. J., Mott, J. M., Lanier, S. H., Williams, W., Ready, D. J., & Teng, E. J. (2012). A pilot study of a 12-week model of group-based exposure therapy for veterans with PTSD. *Journal of Traumatic Stress, 25*(2), 150-156. doi:10.1002/jts.21679

Tran, C. T., Kuhn, E., Walser, R. D., & Drescher, K. D. (2012). The relationship between religiosity, PTSD, and depressive symptoms in veterans in PTSD residential treatment. *Journal of Psychology & Theology, 40*(4), 313-322.

Treatment of Seasonal Affective Disorder (SAD)

Anderson, J. L., Glod, C. A., Dai, J. J., Cao, Y. Y., & Lockley, S. W. (2009). Lux vs. wavelength in light treatment of seasonal affective disorder. *Acta Psychiatrica Scandinavica, 120*(3), 203-212. doi:10.1111/j.1600-0447.2009.01345.x

Dewan, V. K., Sullivan, J. L., & Dewan, I. (2003). Treatment option for seasonal affective disorder. *Canadian Journal of Psychiatry, 48*(8), 572.

Gloth, F.M., Alam, W., & Hollis, B. (1999). Vitamin D vs. broad spectrum phototherapy in the treatment of seasonal affective disorder. *Journal of Nutrition Health and Aging, 3*(1), 5-7.

Golden, R. N., Gaynes, B. N., Ekstrom, R. D., Hamer, R. M., Jacobsen, F. M., Suppes, T., . . . Nemeroff, C.B. (2005). The efficacy of light therapy in the treatment of mood disorders: A review and meta-analysis of the evidence. *The American Journal of Psychology, 162*(4), 656-62.

Lam, R.W. (1998). *Seasonal affective disorder and beyond: Light treatment for SAD and non-SAD conditions.* Arlington, VA: American Psychiatric Publishing.

Mersch, P. P. A., Middendorp, H. M., Bouhuys, A. L., Beersma, D. G. M., & van den Hoofdakker, R. H. (1999). Seasonal affective disorder and latitude: A review of the literature. *Journal of Affective Disorders, 53*(1), 35-48.

Molin, J., Mellerup, E., Bolwig, T., Schieke, T., & Dam, H. (1999). The influence of climate on development of winter depression. *Journal of Affective Disorders, 37*(2-3), 151-155.

Partonen, T., & Lönnqvist, J. (2000). Seasonal affective disorder: A guide to diagnosis and treatment options. In K. J. Palmer, K. J. Palmer (Eds.), *Managing depressive disorders* (pp. 37-47). Kwai Chung, Hong Kong: Adis International Publications.

Rohan, K. J., Roecklein, K. A., Tierney Lindsey, K., Johnson, L. G., Lippy, R. D., Lacy, T. J., & Barton, F. B. (2007). A randomized controlled trial of cognitive-behavioral therapy, light therapy, and their combination for seasonal affective disorder. *Journal of Consulting and Clinical Psychology, 75*(3), 489-500. doi:10.1037/0022-006X.75.3.489

Saha, S., Pariante, C. M., McArdle, T. F., & Fombonne, E. (2000). Very early onset seasonal affective disorder: A case study. *European Child & Adolescent Psychiatry, 9*(2), 135-138.

Sato, T. (1997). Seasonal affective disorder and phototherapy: A critical review. *Professional Psychology: Research and Practice, 28*(2), 164-169. doi:10.1037/0735-7028.28.2.164

Westrin, Å., & Lam, R. W. (2007). Long-term and preventative treatment for seasonal affective disorder. *CNS Drugs, 21*(11), 901-909.

Young, M. A., & Azam, O. A. (2003). Ruminative response style and the severity of seasonal affective disorder. *Cognitive Therapy & Research, 27*(2), 223-232.

Index

"A" paper 25, 27, 30, 33, 39, 47, 65, 75-90
Abbreviations 111
Abstract 78-79, 94-95
Agoraphobia 27, 29
Alphabetical order 34
Anonymous authors 46
As cited in 49-50
Audience 24
Audiovisual media 61-63

"B" paper 25, 27, 66
Bad papers 24
Biased language 69-70
Bipolar disorder 33, 128
Block quotation 47
Blog post 62
Body image 114
Body of paper 29
Books 55-57
Book chapter 56-57
Breakfast 25
Bystander intervention 29, 31, 48, 115

"C" paper 25, 27, 31, 33, 48, 66-67
Case studies 21
Citation 37-50
Claustrophobia 26
Cognitive Behavioral Therapy 33
Comment on blog 63
Compare and contrast 29
Conclusion 32-34
Conformity 39, 48, 116
Context Dependent Memory 15-16, 117
Correlational studies 20
Cracked.com 16

"D" paper 26, 27, 67-68
Depression 27, 129
Dictionaries 59
Direct quotations 46-47, 73
Discussion section 102-103
Dissertation 60

Dissertation abstract 61
DOI numbers 53, 65
DSM-5 59-60

Encyclopedia 58-59
Ethnic groups 70
Exercise and depression 118
Experiments 19
Eyewitness testimony 119

"F" paper 26, 28, 31, 33, 48, 68
Facebook 51, 64
Fonts 107

Gender-biased language 69-70
Generalized Anxiety Disorder 25
Google docs 74
Google Scholar 15, 17

Institutional affiliation 77, 93, 107
In-text citation 37, 40-43
Introduction 25-29, 80-87, 96-97

Journals 52-53

Keywords 78-79

Literaturature reviews 20

Magazines 54
Meetings and symposia 60
Meta-analysis 21
Method section 98-99
Methodological articles 22
Microsoft Word 74
Mnemonics 120
Mood and recall 121
Muller-Lyer illusion 122
Multiple authors 43-44
Munchausen syndrome 26, 28
Music recordings 63
Music video 63

Naps and memory 123
Newspapers 54-55
No author 45-46
No date available 58-59

Obituaries 22
Online dictionary 59
Online encyclopedia 58
Online magazine 54
Online newspaper 55
Online video 63
Outlines 23, 90
Oxford comma 73

Page numbers 108
Page order 108
Paper presentation 60
Paper topics 13
Parenthetical citation 37, 39. 40-46
Periodical (see specific type)
Personal communication 64
PewDiePie 63
Phobias 27, 33, 131
Placebo effect 27, 124
Plagiarism 71-73
Podcast 62
Poster presentation 60
PsycARTICLES 14-15, 17
PsycINFO 14-15, 17
Primary source 18
Psychology databases 14-15, 17
Psychopaths 13

Racial groups 70
Reference section 34-35, 51-64, 88-89, 104-105
Results section 100-101
Reviews 62
Running head 76-77, 92-93, 108

Sample papers 75-105
Seasonal Affective Disorder 30, 47
Secondary source 18

Self-plagiarism 71
Sexual orientation 71
Social media 63-64
Stroop effect 125
Subject-specific book 59-60
Symposia 60

Taylor Swift 62
Technical report 61
Tertiary source 18-19
Textbooks 16-17
Theoretical articles 22
Thesis statement 26-28
Title page 76-77, 92-93
Token economies 25
Treatment of . . .
    ADHD 126
    Alzheimer's 127
    Bipolar 128
    Depression 129
    OCD 130
    Phobias 131
    PTSD 132
    SAD 133
TV shows 62
Twitter 51, 64

Websites 16
Wikipedia 14, 58
Writer's block 23-24

CPSIA information can be obtained
at www.ICGtesting.com
Printed in the USA
LVHW011643120121
676309LV00016B/2253